I0081810

The Flash Point Process

5 Steps to Peace & Fulfillment

Purpose, Direction & Meaning in an Uncertain World

Baxter Castro Coffee

ISBN -10: 0692127291
ISBN-13: 978-0692127292

To Terry L. Mathis

Who first set me on my path to self-discovery.

To my remarkable wife, Vivian

For her loving guidance and support.

To my children, Sarah, Lawrence & Grayson

For believing in me.

"Because a vision softly creeping,
Left its seeds while I was sleeping
And the vision that was planted in my brain
Still remains."

The Sound of Silence, Simon and Garfunkel
Columbia Records, 1964

TABLE OF CONTENTS

PREFACE

Have you reached a point in your life where you long for a clear sense of purpose, direction and meaning? If this is the case, you're not alone. A national, public opinion poll revealed that a staggering 86% of the American population lacks a sense of purpose and meaning in their lives (Barna Group Survey, April 12, 2010). This inability to establish neither purpose nor meaning suggests that many of these individuals also lack a clear sense of direction. This absence of a clear sense of purpose, direction and meaning makes your life incomplete and creates an inner void of Peace& Fulfillment.

My own quest to find a measure of Peace & Fulfillment led to an ongoing spiritual exercise I refer to as my Flash Point Experiment. My purpose for launching this experiment was to try and make my life more balanced and complete to see if this would provide me with a sustainable measure of Peace & Fulfillment. What I have learned from this "Experiment" serves as the basis for this book, and my efforts to teach what I've learned, I refer to as the Flash Point Process. The term, "flash point" can refer to a chemical reaction, as well as *"The point at which something bursts suddenly into being."* Merriam-Webster Dictionary

The purpose of this faith-based book is to help you bring "into being" a sustainable measure of Peace & Fulfillment. The Flash Point Process makes the case that the reason the majority of individuals have difficulty realizing a sustainable measure of Peace & Fulfillment is because there is something missing or not working in their lives. The

Flash Point Process will help you fill this void by challenging you to implement your own Flash Point Experiment.

The Flash Point Process provides a practical, proven guide for those times when you find yourself at a Crossroads of Uncertainty. A "Crossroads of Uncertainty" is any juncture in life when you find yourself at an impasse, crippled by worry, fear or uncertainty, and are unclear about which way to turn or path to take. This impasse could exist when your basic and/or higher needs are not being met, and you don't have the knowledge, skills or experience to get past this juncture. It could also exist when you are disillusioned with a relationship, career or spiritual path or discontented with your current circumstances or station in life. You are at the point where you long for things to change - and change quickly.

The Flash Point Process will help you get past this Crossroads by providing 5-Steps that will enable you to recognize the path or course of action that will provide the life lessons, relationships and experiences you need to establish the purpose, direction and meaning necessary to attain Peace & Fulfillment. This is not a typical self-help book in the sense that it is not a playlist of tips on how to win at the Game of Life. Instead the Flash Point Process will provide a spiritual alternative to this "Game;" one that will encourage you to stop playing this Game altogether, and shift your focus toward making your life more balanced and complete.

The Introduction will provide you with an overview of the Flash Point Process and acquaint you with the Flash Point Experiment. Chapters 1 through 5 will introduce the 5-Steps with their accompanying principles, exercises and ACTION ITEMS. Chapter 6 will share practical, real world applications of the 5-Steps.

The Flash Point Process©

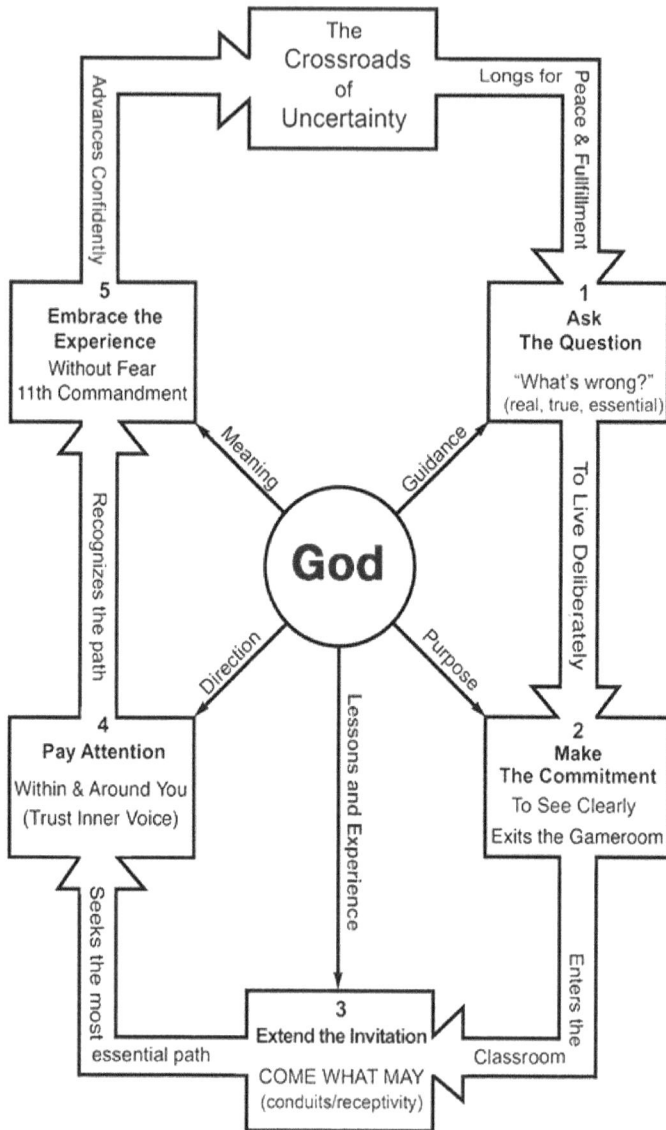

The Crossroads of Uncertainty

Advances Confidently

Longs for Peace & Fulfillment

5
Embrace the Experience
Without Fear
11th Commandment

1
Ask The Question
"What's wrong?"
(real, true, essential)

Meaning

Guidance

To Live Deliberately

God

Recognizes the path

Direction

Purpose

Lessons and Experience

4
Pay Attention
Within & Around You
(Trust Inner Voice)

2
Make The Commitment
To See Clearly
Exits the Gameroom

Seeks the most essential path

3
Extend the Invitation
COME WHAT MAY
(conduits/receptivity)

Classroom

Enters the

Introduction: The Flash Point Process

Why a faith-based path to Peace & Fulfillment? Because you have possibly already exercised your faith, logic and reason and the strength of your will, but have yet to attain a sustainable measure of Peace & Fulfillment. This book will provide the principles, proven tools, skills, and means to fill this void.

Over the past 18 years, we have conducted Flash Point seminars across the country. Our seminar participants often come with a nagging sense of uncertainty, emptiness or discontent with their circumstances or station in life. They long for clarity, certainty and the answer to a one-word question: "HOW?" At least once in their life, every individual would like to experience a sustainable measure of Peace & Fulfillment, but the question always boils down to, How?

These "How" questions can take many forms, but they are generally some variation of, *How do I get from where I am to where I need to be?* Below are some typical "How?" questions that our seminar participants have needed to have answered:

- *How can I know God's Will for my life?*
- *How can I go about establishing a better sense of balance in my life?*
- *How can I acquire a clear sense of purpose, direction and meaning?*
- *How can I find the path or course of action that will provide the experience necessary to attain a sustainable measure of peace and fulfillment?*
- *How do I change the direction in which my life is going?*
- *How can I attain and sustain healthy relationships?*
- *How do I find the means for attaining affordable housing, financial stability, dependable transportation, meaningful work, intellectual land spiritual fulfillment?*
- *How can I overcome my addiction?*

One would think that, after scores of worldwide religions, hundreds of Eastern gurus and New Age mystics, centuries of philosophical ideologies and thousands of self-help books, these HOW? questions would be relatively easy to answer. Apparently not, because the before-mentioned Barna Group survey revealed that 86% of Americans lack a sense of purpose and meaning. In addition, healthcare professionals have documented that the greatest health risks in the workplace today are not physical illness, disease or accidents, but stress and depression - a virtual epidemic of disillusionment and discontent ("Marketplace Stress," Thomas W. Colligan, Eileen M. Higgins, *Journal of Workplace Behavioral Health,* Vol. 21, Issue 2, 2006, pp 89-97). I should also note that in April of 2016, the Center for Disease Control published a report that revealed the suicide rate in America was the highest it's been in 30 years, across all age groups. I wrote this course of instruction to address these How? questions, and in the hope of making a difference in the lives of those affected by these maladies.

Many of our seminar participants have expressed that they have tried to attain Peace & Fulfillment through the accumulation of worldly success, power, position or stockpiling material possessions, but without the desired outcome. It's been my observation that what these individuals are looking for is a new, or at least different set of problem-solving skills and navigational tools, to help them find the path that will provide the experience necessary to attain Peace & Fulfillment. By this I mean the skills and tools they need to get from where they are (at a Crossroads of Uncertainty) to where they need to be (on the path to Peace & Fulfillment).

I mention "uncertainty" because this can be a barrier when trying to establish a sense of purpose, direction and meaning; plus, coping with uncertainty is a constant source of stress in everyone's life. Every day, the media reminds us that we live in uncertain times with lots of problems, roadblocks and challenges to overcome, e.g. we live with threats of nuclear war, international terrorism, corporate downsizing, identify theft, social and political unrest, rampant drug abuse, mass shootings, as well as attacks on the family and the church. The inability to overcome these uncertainties and solve these problems generates stress, fear and worry – all of which contribute to unrest and a void of peace, harmony and fulfillment in our nation, communities, families and individuals.

Anytime you have feelings of uncertainty, disillusionment or discontent, you will experience this void. When you hit a dead-end career, experience a failed relationship, become disillusioned with your spiritual path or facing an insurmountable problem, you will experience a void of Peace & Fulfillment. This void could also exist when your secular or religious beliefs are not providing you with the guidance and direction you need to solve life's problems and challenges, or diminish your fear, worry and uncertainty.

As mentioned, it has been my observation and experience that the most crucial factors that create a void of Peace & Fulfillment is that, there is something missing or not working in your life that is blocking your forward progress.

From my years as a minister, counseling dozens of at-risk populations and hurting individuals, I have learned that most often what is "not working" is that there is something about their thoughts, beliefs, actions, personality and/or lifestyle that is sabotaging their efforts to attain a measure of Peace & Fulfillment. This course of instruction will provide the tools you need to examine and assess those thoughts, beliefs and actions in order to see clearly what it is that has been contributing to your lack of fulfillment. This book will focus on the three most common concerns expressed by our seminar participants: they have a career, relationship or spiritual path that is not working for them. In addition, the Flash Point Process will provide you with the tools you need to attain affordable housing, dependable transportation, good health and financial stability.

I've also learned that often what is "missing" is that your real needs are not being met. Basic needs like the personal growth, spiritual development and physical well-being necessary to have a sense of **balance** in your life, and your higher needs for the sense of purpose, direction and meaning necessary to make your life **complete**.

Personal Growth, Spiritual Development and Physical Well-Being are important because every aspect of your life will fit into one of these three categories, and when you achieve growth and maturity in these basic needs you will have the life balance and clarity of mind to establish your higher needs.

When I use the word, "complete," I mean the attainment of Purpose, Direction and Meaning. You might have achieved, accumulated and accomplished everything you ever wanted and have a life that is full. However, without a sense of purpose, direction and meaning, your life will not be complete. When your life is well-balanced and complete you will have the courage, confidence and skills necessary to attain a sustainable measure of Peace & Fulfilment. In the chapters that follow, this Living Skills course will provide definitions for personal growth, spiritual development, and physical well-being, as well as for purpose, direction and meaning, that are unique to the Flash Point Process. See Figure #1, An Overview of Primessentialism.

Figure #1

Seek first God's Will to help you find the path that will provide the experience necessary to attain Personal Growth, Spiritual Development and Physical Well-Being.

Personal Growth	Spiritual Development	Physical Well-Being
Self-reliance Education Expanded Worldview Relationships Self-knowledge Problem-solving skills	Personal relationship With God Selfless service Prayer Make a difference in the world	Affordable housing Meaningful work Physical fitness Dependable transportation Good health

BALANCE

The attainment of Personal Growth, Spiritual Development and Physical Well-Being brings the life balance and clarity of mind necessary to establish a sense of Purpose, Direction and Meaning.

Purpose – The reason for your journey through life.	Direction – Where your journey is leading you, and the experience it provides.	Meaning – The significance of the life lessons that come with your journey.

↓

COMPLETE

The attainment of Purpose, Direction & Meaning makes your life complete.

↓

PEACE & FULFILLMENT

A life that is balanced and complete will provide a sustainable measure of peace and fulfillment

This course of instruction will also introduce a 5-Step process that will provide the navigational tools you need to get from where you are, to where you need to be, *regardless* of where you are or where you need to be. Mark Twain once observed that, "The secret of getting ahead is getting started." This chapter will help you get started on your path to Peace & Fulfillment by introducing the following:

1. The 5 Themes of Primessentialism
2. A summary of the 5-Steps
3. How to Begin
4. Definitions for the concepts and terms in the chapters that follow
5. The Flash Point Experiment

I certainly don't consider myself an intellectual, theologian or philosopher, but for lack of a better term, the "philosophy" underpinning the Flash Point Process is what I refer to as Primessentialism. The root word for *prime* means "first or best," and the root word for *essential* is "esse" which means, "to be."

Primessentialism
A belief that your most essential path will provide the life lessons, and experience necessary to meet your basic need for personal growth, spiritual development and physical well-being. This in turn, will enable you to establish your higher needs for the sense of purpose, direction and meaning necessary to make your life

**complete. A life that is balanced and complete will provide a
sustainable measure of peace and fulfillment.**

The Five Themes of Primessentialism

1. **To seek first, God's Will,** *will reveal the path that will provide
   the lessons and experiences you need to attain …*
2. **Personal Growth, Spiritual Development and Physical Well-
   Being** *which in turn will provide the life balance necessary to
   establish a …*
3. **Sense of Purpose, Direction and Meaning** *which makes your
   life…*
4. **Whole or Complete** *and from this state of being you will
   experience a …*
5. **Sustainable measure of Peace & Fulfillment** *from one
   Crossroads in life to the next.*

I use the word, "sustainable" because this implies an ongoing, as
opposed to a fleeting measure of Peace & Fulfillment. Financial security,
worldly success and happiness can each provide a measure of Peace &
Fulfillment. However, these are not sustainable because life's
circumstances can change in the "…twinkling of an eye" (1st Corinthians
15:52). This is to say, these have a way of coming and going from year-
to-year, day-to-day and sometimes even hour-by-hour.

The Flash Point Process is designed to be implemented
throughout the course of your life, and as you do, you will attain the
ongoing guidance and direction from God necessary to advance

confidently from one crossroads in life to the next. To facilitate your journey, the Flash Point Process provides the following 5-Steps (Please see the flow chart at the beginning of this chapter):

A Summary of the 5-Steps

Step #1: Ask the Question – How to launch your "Flash Point Experiment" by asking God the following question, *What's wrong with this picture?* The reason for asking this question is to start determining what is missing, wrong or not working in your life. When you ask this "Question" God will start providing the **GUIDANCE** you need to find your next or most essential path(s). You will learn the value of examining the elements that have shaped your Worldview. You will also learn how to create a more balanced life by making the Decision to Live Deliberately. In addition, you will learn how to start identifying your needs and defining clearly the nature of your problem(s) by utilizing the Reality Touchstone to assess objectively your thoughts, beliefs and actions.

Step #2: Make the Commitment – How to cultivate a more credible Worldview by making the Commitment to See Clearly; to see things as they really are instead of how you think they are or want them to be. This commitment will help you to see what you have been thinking, believing or doing that has led you to this particular crossroads in life. You will also learn the value of establishing a sense of **PURPOSE**, the reason for viewing life as God's Classroom without Walls and how to identify any roadblocks that might be blocking your forward progress.

Step #3: Extend the Invitation – Inviting God to send you the **LESSONS and EXPERIENCE** you need from this Classroom brings quickly into being the means to start meeting your needs, solving your problems, and fulfilling your purpose. You will learn how to accelerate this process by dropping your Checklist of Wants & Desires, creating the necessary Conduits of Opportunity" and the receptivity necessary to bring what's needed into being.

Step #4: Pay Attention – How to use the Recognition Factor to discover the path that will provide the experience necessary to attain personal growth, spiritual development and physical well-being. You will learn how to attain a sense of **DIRECTION** by using the navigational tools provided by this chapter and by paying conscious attention to what is taking place within and around you. You will also learn the value of heeding your Internal Guidance System, trusting your Inner Voice, and being mindful of the Perils & Pitfalls of Choice.

Step #5: Embrace the Experience – How to grasp the significance of the people, circumstances and events that come with your path in order to attain a sense of **MEANING** from your life experience. You will learn the value of accepting responsibility for and embracing the lessons, experiences, relationships and solutions that come with any given path in order to learn what they have come to teach you. You will also learn how to sustain your newly found Peace & Fulfillment from one crossroads in life to the next. In addition, I have divided each of the 5-Steps into the following six subsections:

1. Why? - the reasons for initiating each of the 5 Steps

2. My Experience – my personal circumstance or situation that pre-empted each step

3. The Main Ideas - an overview of the key points presented in each chapter

4. What I've Learned - the Primessential Principle upon which each step is based

5. The Question – the question I asked that pre-empted each step

6. The ACTION ITEMS – the four exercises necessary to implement each step

How to Begin

One thing that is unique about this Living Skills course of instruction is the *sequence* in which each step needs to be implemented, as well as how to implement each step. To illustrate this point, we could use the simple example of building a house. All the pieces of a house are important, but in order to achieve the desired outcome, the parts need to be assembled in a pre-established, step-by-step order, beginning with a firm foundation, next the walls and then the roof. The same is true with the Flash Point Process. Its value lies not only in the information presented, but of equal value is the order in which it is presented, e.g. which step to take first, second, third, and so on. I first learned the value of sequential problem-solving as a business consultant, counseling clients who often tried to solve a problem without first going through the sequential steps necessary to identify or define it. Consequently, they often found themselves making mistakes by trying to solve the wrong problem, going in the wrong direction or asking the wrong question.

The secret to avoid making these mistakes is knowing how to begin. Stephen R. Covey, in his book, *The 7 Habits of Highly Effective People*, posited that one of the habits of effective people is to "Begin with the End in Mind." His point being that, when you know exactly what the end result needs to be, it improves greatly the odds of achieving that particular result. Since our end result is to attain a sustainable measure of Peace & Fulfillment, let's begin with the Source you will rely upon for guidance and direction as you make your journey to this end. A primary purpose of this book is to provide a spiritual, as opposed to a secular or rational guide to life. You will begin your Flash Point Experiment by determining which Source you will rely upon for this guidance.

The Source

In the pages that follow, I will share what I have learned from my spiritual Source, coupled with my personal observations and experience. The Flash Point Process makes the basic assumption that such a benevolent Source exits, but this book is not about theology, nor does it offer a rational explanation as to why or how this Source exists. If you are a believer, no explanation is necessary, if you are not a believer, no explanation will suffice. When choosing a name for my own Source I use the word God. I use the masculine pronoun "he" when referring to God simply because the scriptures teach that when we pray, we should address God as "our father" (Matthew 6:9).

I define this Source as, *That entity from which all truth and being emanates.* What the philosopher Paul Tillich called, "The ground of Being." The religious individual might refer to his or her Source as God, Jesus, Heavenly Father, God, Yahweh, Krishna or Allah. For those individuals who are "unchurched," religiously unaffiliated, or see their path as spiritual instead of religious, they might call their source the Supreme Being, Higher Power, Cosmic Consciousness or simply the Universe. Still others might draw upon secular ideologies, astrology or Eastern mysticism as their Source for guidance and direction. As to which Source is right or best, I leave this for the individual reader to determine for his or herself. I've learned that,

The nature and quality of my life I experience is directly proportional to the credibility of the Source upon which I rely to bring this experience into being.

The Inner Voice

"There is always one true inner voice. Trust it." Gloria Steinem, *Revolution From Within*

I would suggest that everyone has access to their Inner Voice. Some individuals ignore this voice, others have yet to tap into this voice, and still others have been guided by this voice all of their lives. When an individual tunes-in to their Source, it provides him or her access to their Inner Voice. One way to view the dynamic of the Inner Voice is to picture your Source as the broadcasting entity, and your heart, mind and soul as the collective receiver. Tuning-in to this Inner Voice can provide the guidance and direction necessary to recognize the path or course of action that will meet your career, relationship and spiritual needs. See Chapter 5 for additional insights about this Inner Voice.

The Flash Point Experiment

In the first of the 5-Steps, the Flash Point Process will challenge you to launch what I refer to as a Flash Point Experiment. The purpose of this "Experiment" is threefold. First, to make your life more balanced by providing you with the exercises and skills you need to attain personal growth, spiritual development and physical well-being. Second, to provide you with the navigational tools necessary to recognize the path that will provide the life lessons, relationships and experience necessary to meet all your needs. And third, to establish the sense of purpose, direction and meaning necessary to make your life complete.

For your particular experiment, I suggest you set aside a 90-day period of time in order to apply the 5-Steps to finding the life lessons and experiences you need. Most of my readers will begin seeing differently themselves, life and others within the first 90 days of starting their experiment. Psychologists have determined that it takes 28 days to change a habit. However, I have learned from experience that 90 days is a more realistic timeframe for this "experiment" because this allows for any missteps or false starts. When you implement your experiment, it will be a deliberate act that says you're willing to pay the price in time and effort to determine what is missing or not working in your life.

In summary, the Flash Point Process will provide the means to attain balance in your life, offer a proven, faith-based problem-solving model, as well as the skills and exercises necessary to establish a sense of

Purpose, Direction and Meaning on your path to Peace & Fulfillment. This book is not so much an attempt to present something new, but simply to provide a systematic course of instruction that will provide the skills and tools necessary to solve your problems, meet your basic and higher needs, overcome your fear worry and uncertainty, and fill your void of Peace & Fulfilment.

A Few End Notes

I acknowledge beforehand that there is a good deal of repetition in this course of instruction. I have done this intentionally because from my days as a college professor and as a minister, I have learned the value of repetition. Subsequently, I will present the same material, but from different vantage points, and with different anecdotes, in order to increase the odds of any one individual internalizing a given concept or principle.

I have alternated between genders in every other chapter to avoid the tedious use of he/she or his/hers. This is a faith-based book, but not centered around any given theology. One last note - unless otherwise noted, all scriptures quoted are from the King James Version of the Bible.

Perhaps you have reached a crossroads in life and are uncertain about which way to turn or which path to take. I suggest that before you begin your Flash Point Experiment you make a list of at least three How? questions that are the most pressing in your life today. This list might include a relationship, career or spiritual challenge, or you might be facing a financial, health, housing or transportation crisis. In addition, you might be disillusioned or discontented with your existing circumstance or station in life, and you long for immediate change.

Now that you have an overview of the Flash Point Process, Chapter 1 will facilitate your efforts to launch your Flash Point Experiment.

Step #1: Ask the Question

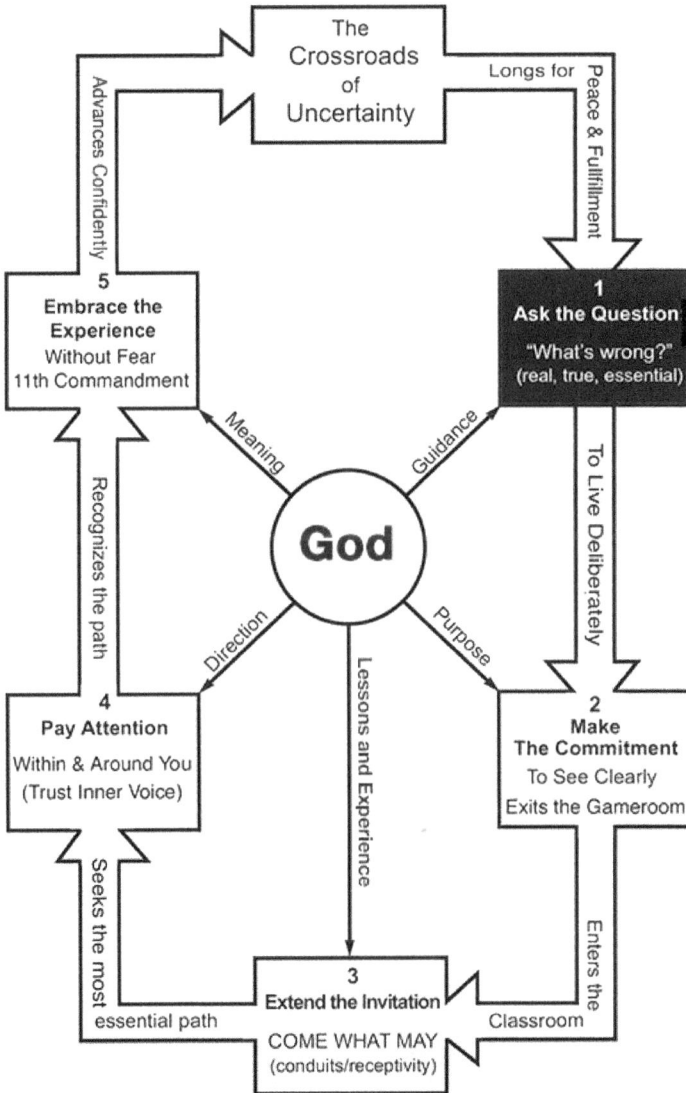

The
Crossroads
of
Uncertainty

Longs for

Peace & Fulfillment

Advances Confidently

5
Embrace the
Experience
Without Fear
11th Commandment

1
Ask the Question
"What's wrong?"
(real, true, essential)

To Live Deliberately

Meaning

Guidance

God

Recognizes the path

Direction

Purpose

Lessons and Experience

4
Pay Attention
Within & Around You
(Trust Inner Voice)

2
Make
The Commitment
To See Clearly
Exits the Gameroom

Seeks the most

Enters the

3
Extend the Invitation
COME WHAT MAY
(conduits/receptivity)

essential path

Classroom

Chapter 1

Step One: Ask the Question

ASK THE QUESTION – Ask God, *What's wrong with this picture; what's missing or not working that's creating this void of Peace & Fulfillment in my life?* To ask this question creates the longing necessary to begin filling this void, acknowledges there is something in your life that's sabotaging your efforts to attain this Peace & Fulfillment, and launches your Flash Point Experiment.

"From a certain point onward, there is no longer any turning back. That is the point that must be reached." Franz Kafka, Czechoslovakian novelist

A. WHY ASK THE QUESTION?

- Because at least once in their life, every individual has reached a point where he finds himself standing at a Crossroads of Uncertainty, and unclear about which way to turn or which path to take. This point comes when you find yourself facing a difficult or what appears to be an insurmountable challenge or problem, one for which you lack the skills, tools or experience to solve.

- In addition, you might find yourself at this crossroads due to your dissatisfaction with a personal relationship, disillusionment with your career or spiritual path, or discontentment with your current circumstances or station in life.

- Perhaps you have reached the point where you want to know which of your thoughts, beliefs and/or actions have led you to this particular Crossroads, as well as the elements that have shaped those thoughts and beliefs and influenced those actions.

- You might not have the tools necessary to assess accurately and objectively your ideas, beliefs and actions. How the absence of these tools could be blocking your efforts to find the path(s) that will provide the experiences necessary to attain personal growth, spiritual development and physical well-being.

When you ask God, *What's wrong with this picture?* it creates a deep-felt longing to fill the void of Peace & Fulfillment in your life and launches your Flash Point Experiment. When you "Ask the Question," you are acknowledging that there is something missing or not working in your life. You are weary of uncertainty, discontent and disillusionment - you long for change and a way to experience life, if not perfectly, then at least differently

B. MY EXPERIENCE - My personal world collapsed at the age of 41. I refer to this disaster as my Great Train Wreck because over the course of nine months, I simultaneously lost my family, my business, all my money, my health and even my religion. You might have experienced a similar disaster when you went through a difficult divorce, a business failure, experienced a bankruptcy or derailed your life through the abuse of drugs or alcohol.

Chapter 3 will be the more appropriate place to summarize the events that led up to this Train Wreck. For now, let me simply say that it was a major crossroads in my life, and because of these life-altering disasters, I had many unanswered questions:

- *Does everyone have to make a complete wreck of their lives before they take stock of their thoughts, beliefs and actions, or is it just me?*
- *How did my life get so out of balance?*
- *Why is this happening to me, what did I do wrong?*

- *How do I get out of this dilemma?*
- *What do I need to think, see and do differently?*
- *How do I change my circumstances and station in life?*
- *How do I determine God's Will for my life?*

After my Great Train Wreck, I found myself grappling with these kinds of questions for more than a year. At that point it occurred to me that the reason I wasn't getting any answers was because I either didn't really want to know those answers or I was asking the wrong questions. It was at that point I asked God, *What's wrong with this picture?* When I asked that particular question, it was as if a light bulb had switched on in my brain. I didn't have a clue as to how I was going to get my life back on track. At that point, I realized that my life had become a complete train wreck, totally lacking any real sense of purpose, direction or meaning.

It had become glaringly obvious to me that I had somehow missed what was essential to experience a successful and meaningful life, and there needed to be some kind of fundamental change in the way I had been thinking, believing and acting. In addition, because I had lost so much as a result of this Train Wreck, I felt I needed to find an alternate way to meet my need for affordable housing, dependable transportation, meaningful work, financial stability, and spiritual fulfillment Although I had no idea where to begin, there was no doubt in my mind that I was at a pivotal crossroads in life. I knew that it was time for a change. Not a minor change, but a major shift in my perception of reality (my Worldview), i.e. how I saw myself, my relationships, my career, my religion and life in general. My longing to make this change is what fueled my Flash Point Experiment.

The "How?" question I needed to answer was, "How do I begin the journey that will take me from where I am - standing at The Crossroads of Uncertainty, to where I need to be - on the path to Peace & Fulfillment?"

C. The MAIN IDEAS – Chapters 1 and 2 will help you to start identifying your needs, defining your problems and establishing a sense of PURPOSE. Chapters 3-5 will help you meet your needs, solve those problems, fulfill that purpose and establish a sense of DIRECTION and MEANING. Perhaps you find yourself at a Crossroads of Uncertainty, and have done all you can think of to get past this point, but you are at a loss as to which way to turn or path to take. Step 1 will address this concern by encouraging you to begin your 90-day Flash Point Experiment by asking God the following question: *What's Wrong with This Picture?* The reason for asking this question is to seek God's guidance while trying to identify and meet your needs, define and solve your problems as well as determine what's missing or not working in your life. Step 1 will also provide you with the tools you need to assess the credibility of the elements that have shaped your perception of reality and how this Worldview could be hampering your efforts to attain a sustainable measure of Peace & Fulfillment.

Let's begin by defining what constitutes an experiment. The Merriam-Webster Dictionary defines an experiment as, "A trial, process or procedure undertaken for the purpose of discovering something unknown or testing a principle." The "process" will be the 5-Steps of the Flash Point Process. What you will be "discovering" is the path that will provide the life lessons and experience that are most essential for your personal growth, spiritual development and physical well-being. What you will be "testing" are the Primessential Principles introduced in the "What I've Learned" section of this and subsequent chapters.

The purpose of this experiment is to discover the path(s) or course of action that will provide the experience necessary to meet all your needs. I put "path(s)" in parentheses because there will be times when you are seeking a singular path, and there will be other times when you will be pursuing multiple paths, e.g. a career, relationship, spiritual path, etc. These needs include the basic need for the personal growth, spiritual development and physical well-being necessary to have a healthy life balance. In the pages to follow, we will discuss why it's necessary to pursue these basic needs before pursuing your higher needs for the purpose, direction and meaning necessary to make your life complete.

As you begin your Flash Point Experiment, I would like to extend a cautionary note. This experiment is not for the faint of heart because your experiment will require a great deal of self-reflection and hard work. It will challenge you to trust in God, and be completely open to change, as well as exercise honesty, integrity and fierce individualism on your journey. I mention this because many of our seminar participants have said they really want their lives to change. However, when it comes down to critically examining their situation, thoughts and beliefs, and questioning their actions, they often tend to make excuses for their situation, self-justify those thoughts and beliefs, and defend those actions.

The Flash Point Process is designed to facilitate a journey that will take you from where you are (feeling lost and unfulfilled) to where you need to be (a fulfilling and meaningful life). This journey begins by pursuing the **First Theme of Primessentialism,** which is to include the search for God's Will as you seek the life lessons and experience necessary for meeting your needs. There are any numbers of ways that the term "God's Will" could be defined, described or interpreted. For the purposes of the Flash Point Process, when we use this term, we are suggesting that God exists and is a personal God who provides individual guidance and direction to help us find our way through life. We further suggest that his "Will" is for us to experience the life lessons and relationships that are most essential for us to attain personal growth, spiritual development and physical well-being.

When we suggest you seek first God's Will this is not to say that God has a specific career, relationship or spiritual path you should pursue. It's just that, there are 1,000s of paths and possibilities you could pursue, and there will be some, more than others, that will be essential for your personal growth, spiritual development and physical well-being. Seeking guidance and direction from God will help you avoid those paths and possibilities that would only bring heartache, disillusionment or discontent.

The dictionary defines the word *seek* as, "To try to find something by looking or otherwise seeking carefully and thoroughly." There are two key points to seeking "carefully and thoroughly." The first point is to exercise the fierce individualism necessary to find your own path through life, without relying on your family, cultural conditioning or the unrealistic social conventions and expectations of others to dictate your path.

The second, and very key point, is to keep a *very* open mind, without clinging to any preconceived ideas you might have about what *should* constitute God's Will or a meaningful life.

The scriptures teach that we ultimately find some version of that which we truly seek. Matthew 7:7 Consequently, to the degree that you seek "carefully and thoroughly," to that same degree will you find the path that leads to a fulfilling life. To seek first, God's Will means to stop being a Follower and start becoming a Seeker. You stop following, and start questioning, the influence of others, e.g. family and peers, popular opinion, as well as any misguided expectations from your religious and educational institutions. In addition, you start questioning your own thoughts, beliefs and actions, and stop following blindly the social conventions, cultural conditioning and expectations of those who have a preconceived idea about how you should be living your life, i.e. how you should think, believe and act. What you start seeking is the path that will provide you with the life lessons, relationships and experience God knows are most essential for meeting your real needs and fulfilling his Will. I use the term, "real needs" to differentiate between one's worldly wants and desires. Worldly wants and desires are those things we have been culturally conditioned to pursue, e.g. power, position, prestige and possessions, luxury cars, stately houses, expensive clothes and jewelry, exotic vacations, etc.

Another reason for seeking first, God's Will is that he will lead you to the path that will provide the experience necessary to realize the **Second Theme of Primessentialism,** which is to attain the Personal

Growth, Spiritual Development and Physical Well-Being necessary to realize a well-balanced life. This is necessary because the solutions to all your problems will come from one or more of these three categories. In addition, every aspect of your life will fall into one of these three categories and each has a direct bearing on the nature and quality of your life experience. As your life becomes more rounded and well balanced, you will begin to establish a reason or *purpose f*or this effort, a *direction* that will provide the experience necessary to facilitate this effort, and the level of *meaning* it takes to make sense of this experience. The primary purpose of this chapter is to provide you with the skills, tools and ideas necessary to launch your Flash Point Experiment by encouraging you to:

- Identify your needs and define the problems you will encounter on your journey (WHAT I'VE LEARNED).
- Establish who and what it is that you truly long for on this journey (The QUESTION).
- Critically examine and question the elements whose influence has led you to your current crossroads in life. (ACTION ITEM #1 & 2)
- Make the Decision to Live Deliberately (ACTION ITEM #3).
- Utilize the "Reality Touchstone" to assess the credibility of your thoughts, beliefs and actions. (ACTION ITEM #4)

D. WHAT I'VE LEARNED – *The answer to every problem is*

inherent in the problem itself. The more clearly defined the problem the more self-evident the solution. "If I had 60 minutes to solve a problem, I'd spend 55 minutes defining it, and 5 minutes solving it." Albert Einstein, Noble prize-winning physicist

Have you ever said to yourself, *I know what my problems are, I just don't know how to solve them.* Our response to this statement is that there is a high probability that you can't find the solutions you seek because you have yet to define honestly, objectively and/or clearly those problems. This can happen when you don't know how to identify those problems, or as sometimes is the case, you don't want to identify the real problem. This **1st Primessential Principle** suggests that, you can't meet a need you can't identify or solve a problem you can't define. It further suggests that once you have accurately identified and defined your needs and problem(s), the solutions will often be self-evident.

For example, if I only said that my stomach hurt, this might not define my problem clearly enough for you to solve it because my problem could be appendicitis, stomach cramps, intestinal flu, cancer, etc. However, if I redefined my stomach problem as simply being hungry, the solution would be self-evident. You could then think of all kinds of creative and affordable solutions to this particular problem. The sooner you can determine exactly what it is you are missing, doing, thinking or believing that is blocking your forward progress, the sooner you can change the nature and quality of your life experience.

The reason this 1st Primessential Principle is crucial to the success of your Flash Point Experiment is that the path to a meaningful life can be fraught with a wide range of problems to solve and roadblocks to overcome. If you lack effective problem-solving skills, you will need to acquire some new skills. New problem-solving skills will require a new or different perception of reality – a different way of viewing life and a different way of looking at yourself, situations and others.

The first step toward identifying your needs and defining your problem(s) is to "begin with the end in mind" by determining exactly who and what it is you are searching for over the course of your Flash Point Experiment.

E. THE QUESTION - *Who or what do I truly long for?* – "Feeling and longing are the motive forces behind all human endeavor and human creations." Albert Einstein

As you find yourself at this particular crossroads in life, you might not have any idea about who or what it is that you should now be longing or searching for. The reason we suggest you ask yourself, *What do I truly long for?* is to provide you with an exercise that will enable you to focus better on what you are looking for in life.

Your longing fuels your efforts and creates the receptivity necessary to bring into being what or whom you need. Consequently, the more clearly you understand whom or what it is you long for, the more likely you are to attract, attain or achieve it.

At the beginning of our seminars we ask our participants if they long for Peace & Fulfillment, and they invariably say, "Yes." However, *before* we ask this question, we ask them to write down exactly what it is they long for in their lives, and the most frequent answers we get are along the lines of:

- I long to be happy
- I long to be successful
- I long for things to be different
- I long for the American Dream
- I long to be rich
- I long for my circumstances or station in life to change

Unfortunately, many people believe that if they are happy, successful or living the American Dream this will meet their needs. However, happiness can be fleeting, riches can come and go, and change just for the sake of change will not bring fulfillment. In addition, success in a worldly sense might make your life full, but it will not be complete until you discover God's Will for your life. By "worldly success" I mean those things we have been culturally conditioned to seek, e.g. riches, power, position, material possessions, fame, recognition or the perfect companion, career, car or house.

Jean Nidetch, the woman who started the highly successful Weight Watchers program, once remarked that when she finally realized that what she longed for wasn't food, she was able to start losing weight. In other words, it's only when you understand exactly who or what it is you are hungry for will you bring into being the means to attain it. If you can't or don't want to determine exactly what or whom it is you long for you will have to settle for whatever or whomever you can get.

As you begin your Flash Point Experiment, take a moment to reflect on who or what it is you truly long for. When you do this, I suggest you draw a vertical line down the middle of a clean sheet of paper, creating two columns on the page. On the top of the left column, write the title, My List of Wants & Desires. In the left column, make a list of *who or what you want and desire*, e.g. riches, power, position, the perfect companion, etc. You could also list the material things you want or desire, e.g. luxury homes and cars, expensive jewelry, fashionable clothes, exotic vacations, etc. On the top of the right column, write the title, My List of Needs. In the right column, make a list of *what you need* out of life, e.g. your need for personal growth, spiritual development and physical well-being as well as a sense of purpose, direction and meaning. You could also add to this list your need for good health, financial stability, affordable housing, further education, dependable transportation, intellectual and spiritual fulfillment, etc.

The reason for this exercise is twofold. The first reason is to begin distinguishing between your worldly wants and desires versus your most essential needs. This is a theme that will recur throughout this course of instruction. There's nothing wrong with pursuing worldly wants and desires as long as you keep in mind that these wants and desires are largely fueled by vanity, ego or the desire for power, position or possessions or wanting to live up to the social conventions and cultural expectations of others. The second reason is that you will not be able to find your next or most essential path if you don't know whom or what you are looking for, or what needs you have that need to be met.

F. THE ACTION ITEMS - "To be nobody-but-yourself in a world which is doing its best, night and day, to make you everybody else, means to fight the hardest battle which one human being can fight; and never stop fighting." E. E. Cummings, *A Poet's Advice to Students*

The ACTION ITEMS in this chapter will facilitate your efforts to launch your Flash Point Experiment. It begins by getting in touch with your authentic or True Self, examining the elements that have shaped that Self, and then questioning what might be inaccurate or distorted about your perception of reality (your Worldview). In addition, these ACTION ITEMS will provide the skills you need to start determining what's not working or missing in your life, as well as the tools to start identifying your needs and defining your problems.

Your Flash Point Experiment begins with the concept of Self, and for a very important reason. It's only your authentic or "True Self" that can chart a path to the life, relationships and experience that will meet the needs unique to your particular circumstances or station in life. No one else can do this for you. If you seek someone else's path, you will only find someone else's experience. Someone else's experience will never meet your own needs and will always lead to discontent or disillusionment. "To be yourself in a world that is constantly trying to make you something else is the greatest accomplishment." Ralph Waldo Emerson, *Essays*

Your Flash Point Experiment will encourage you to be

"…nobody-but-yourself." By True Self, I mean your inner or core Self, minus the influence of your family and religion, your cultural conditioning, and the "shoulds" and expectations of others. Because attaining a true sense of this Self is so critical to the success of your Experiment, let's digress for a moment, and explore this concept.

Eric Fromm, in his book, *The Art of Loving*, referred to this "Self" as, "A core in our personality which is unchangeable and which persists throughout our life in spite of varying circumstances, and regardless of certain changes in opinions and feelings." In other words, your True Self is not the sum total of your education, religious beliefs, travels or career; these are merely things that have been added to your True Self over the course of your life. The primary reason for getting in touch with your core or True Self is that only a True Self can have a Credible Worldview. It's only with a Credible Worldview that you can recognize the path that God has provided for the life lessons and experience necessary to meet your needs (See Chapter 2 for more on this Credible Worldview).

As a professional artist, perhaps I could illustrate the concept of authentic or true by drawing from art history. One of the things that make for great and lasting art is not because it's new or different, but because it is authentic. Its greatness comes from its integrity and originality, and these come from its authenticity. When I use the term, *authentic,* I mean that it is not influenced or defined by someone else's art, nor is it based on other peoples' expectations of what art should be. As you launch your Flash Point Experiment, you will no longer settle for having the content of your True Self influenced or defined by how others think it should be, because you have already followed that path, and it didn't lead to peace or fulfillment.

It's been said that, *You don't have to be who you have become, but you can be who you are.* Why is it necessary to "be who you are"? Because,

The vast majority of individuals are not conscious of the fact that, for much of their lives, they have been living someone else's version of their life.

When you live someone else's version of your life you are in effect, living someone else's version of your Self. A version created by striving to please somebody, "everybody else," and trying to live up to their expectations (family, peers, church, popular culture, etc.). These external expectations don't encourage you to be your Ture Self, but subtly and not so subtly pressure you to conform - to think, believe and act like everybody else. "Your time is limited, so don't waste it living someone else's life." Steve Jobs, founder of Apple Computer

I can speak from first-hand experience what it is like to live someone else's version of one's life. From my youth I lived my parents' version of my life. I had my hair cut as I was supposed to. I wore the clothes I was expected to wear. I accepted without question their rules, beliefs, traditions and values, and behaved in a way that was expected of me. In my early teens, I fabricated another version of my Self. I wanted to be popular so I created a "popular version" of my Self. This fabricated version required me to act how popular people *should* act and participate in the *right* school activities and hang out with the *acceptable* crowd. At the age of 21, I converted to a new religion. Subsequently, I began living its version of my life – to dress, act, think and believe like I was *supposed* to in order to stand in good fellowship with that church. However, it wasn't until 20 years later, when I began my Flash Point Experiment, that I decided I was weary of living everyone else's version of my life. I simply needed to be myself in a world that was relentlessly trying to make me like "everybody else." Since the concept of self is critical to the success of your Flash Point Experiment, let's examine three possible versions of this Self:

- **Your Envisioned Self** – This is whom you want to believe you are. It's how you see yourself; the image of yourself you want to think is authentic, but can be tainted by pride, ego, vanity and self-deception.

- **Your Fabricated Self** - Whom others think you are. It's an affectation, the different parts of yourself that you have revealed to your friends, a different self to your boss and coworkers, and possible another Fabricated Self to your church family.

- **Your True or Authentic Self** – The very core of your being; your eternal self. This is who you really are - minus the cultural labels, class distinctions, social conventions and the well-intentioned, but often misguided expectations of others.

In the words of the anthropologist, Margaret Mead, "Often people attempt to live their lives backwards; they try to have more things or more money in order to do more of what they want, so they will be happier. The way it actually works is the reverse. You must first be who you really are, then do what you need to do, in order to have what you want."

This journey to becoming "who you really are" in a world that is trying to "make you everybody else" can be a challenge because who and what you have become has been greatly influenced by the external elements that have shaped your perception of reality from childhood. Before you begin your experiment, it will be necessary to determine the credibility of this perception of reality by examining and questioning each of these elements. These elements constitute what I refer to as one's Database of Knowledge & Experience.

ACTION ITEM #1: Examine Your Database of Knowledge & Experience - "For man, the unexamined life is not worth living." Socrates

The purpose of this ACTION ITEM is to encourage you to examine, question and reflect on the external elements that have shaped your perception of reality, and how this reality has led you to this particular crossroads in life.

As mentioned, your perception of reality is often referred to as your Worldview, i.e. your thoughts, beliefs and understanding of how things are or should be. From behavioral science, we have learned that one's thoughts and beliefs determine their actions, which have some kind of consequence. However, in order to bring about real change, you will need to go further upstream to identify the elements that have shaped those thoughts and beliefs. In order to accomplish this, you will need to examine and question the credibility of the 4 Elements that constitute your personal Database of Knowledge & Experience.

Your Database of Knowledge & Experience shapes your Worldview (your ideas, thoughts and beliefs). This Worldview, or perception of reality, is the driving force behind your actions and behaviors which result in some kind of outcome or consequence. This outcome will then reinforce, challenge or threaten the information in your Database of Knowledge & Experience. See Figure #2: "The Mechanics of Cause & Effect":

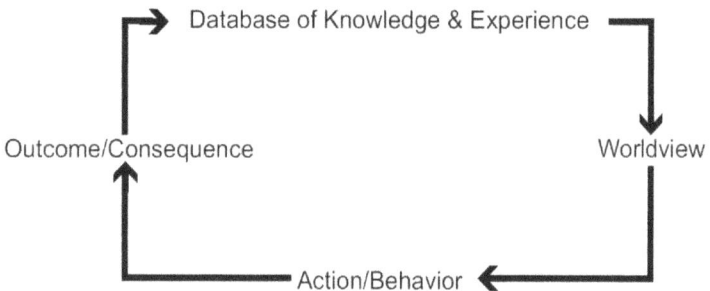

Figure #2

The Mechanics of Cause & Effect

Database of Knowledge & Experience

Outcome/Consequence   Worldview

Action/Behavior

One way to begin answering the question, "What's wrong with this picture?" is to examine the reliability and credibility of the 4 Elements that comprise your Database of Knowledge & Experience. These 4 Elements are the sources for everything you have learned. (See Figure #3):

Figure #3

The 4 Elements

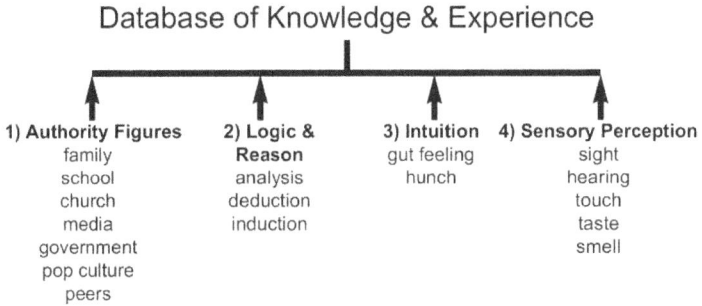

Database of Knowledge & Experience

1) Authority Figures	2) Logic & Reason	3) Intuition	4) Sensory Perception
family	analysis	gut feeling	sight
school	deduction	hunch	hearing
church	induction		touch
media			taste
government			smell
pop culture			
peers			

I would suggest that each of the 4 Elements that make up this Database of Knowledge & Experience form a kind of box. This "box" is your Worldview, your own unique perception of reality - how you think and believe life is or how you want or expect it to be (See Figure #4):

Figure #4

Your Worldview

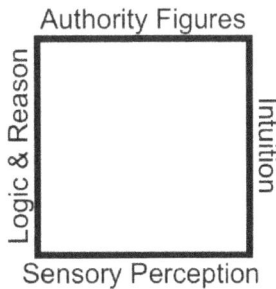

Authority Figures

Logic & Reason

Intuition

Sensory Perception

We have all heard the expression, "Think outside the box." It is a key premise of Primessentialism that it is not actually possible to think outside this "box" since this box consists of the 4 Elements that have shaped your personal Worldview. In other words, it's not possible to think outside one's existing perception of reality. However, it is possible to expand the dimensions of this reality by incorporating new ideas, relationships, perspectives, information and experience into your Database of Knowledge & Experience.

Examining Your Database of Knowledge & Experience

It is critical to the success of your Flash Point Experiment to doubt, examine or at least question the credibility of the elements that have shaped your Worldview. What I am suggesting is that you question everything you've thought, believed or have been told about life. I suggest this because, if you are having difficulty attaining or sustaining a measure of Peace & Fulfillment, there is a high probability that there is something about your perception of reality that is creating this difficulty. The French philosopher Rene Descartes believed that, "If you would be a real seeker of truth, it is necessary that at least once in your life you doubt, as far as possible, all things."

If you proceed with your Flash Point Experiment without first questioning the credibility of the elements that comprise your Database of Knowledge & Experience, you might be viewing life and relationships through a distorted Worldview. I've learned that,

Without an accurate perception of reality, I will not be able to recognize the path that will provide the experience and life lessons I need to make my life balanced and complete.

When I use the term "life lessons," I am referring to everything you need to learn about life, e.g. health, finance, science, relationships, trust, responsibility, education, love, religion, the world of work, the humanities, etc. As you begin to question these four elements, let's examine briefly how each could contribute to the accuracy or distortion of your Worldview.

a. Authority Figures – The authority figures in your life provide your first introduction to the social norms and cultural conditioning you will encounter throughout your life, i.e. how others expect you to think, believe and act. I write at length about authority figures because they have had the greatest influence on our perceptions of reality. Subsequently, the accuracy of your Worldview is heavily dependent on the credibility of this influence. This influence comes to you in the form of peer, religious, cultural and family beliefs, rules, maxims and traditions you've heard so many times that you assume they are valid, but in fact they might not be. What I am suggesting is that, once you have reached adulthood, it is ok to examine and question the influence of your authority figures, e.g. their values, traditions, rules, expectations and beliefs.

A critical examination of what we have been taught by our parents can be a daunting task, because when we are born, we are completely dependent on our parents to meet our needs for food, shelter and clothing, as well as to teach us what is good, right and acceptable. Most individuals stay in their parent's home until they become young adults. Consequently, as children, they have had the traditions, rules, values and beliefs of their parents reinforced continuously over the course of many years. As is often the case, our parents condition us not to question their values, traditions, rules and beliefs. If those traditions, rules and beliefs are credible, it creates a Worldview that will result in the child growing up well-adjusted and prepared for life, love, career and their spiritual path. If those ideas and beliefs are biased, distorted or untrue, the child will find adult life and decision-making very daunting, if not overwhelming.

We encounter our second set of authority figures when we start to school. At school, we learn what to think and how to act from our teachers as well as the social rules we learn from our fellow classmates on the playground. In Michael Samuel's book, *Seeing with the Mind's Eye,* he relates a story about children in a kindergarten class. The teacher instructed the children to draw a bird from their imagination. Each child proceeded to draw a highly original and creative interpretation of a bird. The next day the children were given a coloring book, and were instructed to use their crayons to "color five birds" shaped liked the letter V. On the third day, their teacher again asked them to draw a picture of a bird from their imagination. The children believed that the right way to draw a bird was to imitate what had been presented by their authority figure (the teacher). Subsequently, each child proceeded to draw a bird shaped like the letter V instead of drawing a bird from their individual imaginations. In other words, the children were now programmed or culturally conditioned to rely on this authority figure to show them how things are - how the drawing of a bird *should* look. This institutional programming continues from kindergarten through adult life.

In addition to home and school, many of our parents took us to church, temple, mosque, or synagogue, where we encountered a third set of authority figures in the form of priests, rabbis, mullahs, and pastors. These authority figures taught us creeds, moral codes and what constitutes appropriate thoughts, beliefs and behaviors. Credible religious instruction can be very beneficial, but it has been my observation that many religious institutions rarely encourage their members to look outside their particular religion for God's Will or reality and truth. If the thoughts and beliefs of your authority figures dominate your thinking, this can result in a limited, if not distorted, perception of reality. A distorted perception of reality will not enable you to see clearly your next or most essential path(s) through life.

By the time we reach our teenage years, we do start to think for ourselves, but at that point we face an even more daunting set of authority figures. These include our peers who influence our choice of friends and includes our first real introduction to members of the opposite sex, as well as how we should think or act in order to conform to the various cliques that come with this age, e.g. the "brainiacs," the jocks, the nerds, the preppies, the gangs, etc. Unfortunately, since all youth are still in their narcissistic, formative years, their influence, opinions and judgments can be harsh, critical, superficial and not always grounded in reality or truth. This superficial influence could cause a young person to develop a distorted Worldview, which in turn could negatively affect his self-image and hamper his ability to experience a fulfilling life. For instance, we could use the example of the "ugly duckling syndrome." I have met a number of women who were teased throughout their childhood for being less than physically attractive. However, when these women reached adulthood they were physically transformed into beautiful women. Unfortunately, for many of these women, they continue to see themselves as ugly ducklings instead of beautiful swans because this self-image was established in their youth.

Upon becoming young adults, we are confronted with new kinds of authority figures in the form of popular culture, e.g. television personalities, rock stars, social media, supermarket tabloids, movie stars, shock jocks, Internet celebrities, professional athletes, etc. The influence of these role models is trendy, fashionable, generational and often unreliable because fads, trends and celebrities come and go, and popular opinion can be very fickle about what constitutes success and a meaningful life. In addition to our peers, popular culture's influence extends to what constitutes a *perfect* life. In other words, we are culturally conditioned as to what kind of life, career, religion or companion we should seek. This in turn, leads to a lot of disappointing outcomes when we can't establish a life that measures up to those unrealistic expectations.

As adults, we encounter yet another other set of authority figures. We have to learn the social skills, traditions and rules necessary to fit-in with our neighbors, fellow church members, employers and colleagues who can bring pressure as to what we "should" think, act or believe. This often leads to political, social and religious conformity for the sake of fitting in. To examine the credibility of the influence from popular culture and your authority figures, ask yourself, "What's wrong with this picture – how much of what have I been told, and led to believe about life, love and religion is in fact, invalid, untrue or distorted?"

b. Logic & Reason - Logic and reason are essential because inductive and deductive reasoning provide the primary tools for analyzing facts and solving problems. For example, if your thinking is logically dominant, you might justify dating only someone who logically fits your image of the ideal companion, e.g. physically attractive, blond hair, blue eyes, worldly successful, etc. You seek this because this is what you most want or desire in a relationship. However, what might be closer to fulfillment would be to find a companion using less superficial criteria, e.g. someone who is a hard worker, loving, nurturing, creative, has shared values, is spiritual and intelligent, and meets your needs instead of fulfilling your desires.

Another major, but often-overlooked limitation of logic and reason, is that they are both the product of left-brain dominant, abstract thinking. Without a balance of right-brain dominant, concrete thinking, it is difficult to see the big picture, which creates a Worldview that can't see the forest for the trees. Left-brain thinking uses logic, reason, critical thinking and analysis to process facts and information. Left-brain dominant thinking asks questions like, *What are the facts about this situation or person?* Right-brained dominant thinking uses their emotions and creative, big picture, conceptual thinking to understand not only what is there, but also to grasp what is not there. Right-brain thinking asks questions like, *What is this situation or person about and what does that mean?*

A balance of left and right brain-dominant thinking enables you to see both, the forest *and* the trees - the ability to grasp the big picture and understand what it means. The limitations of left-brain dominance are noteworthy because sociologists have determined that 88% of the American population consists of left-brained dominant, analytical thinkers. These individuals have little or no training on how to balance left and right brain thinking, and therefore they have a limited, if not distorted, perception of reality.

Since the overwhelming majority of our population has this distorted perception of life, it's easy to see how the reality constructed by this majority would be less than accurate. This in turn makes an excellent case for not buying-in to everything or anything you've been told about how life should be. Ask yourself, "Am I justifying this course of action because it's the most logical fit or because it meets my real needs?"

c. Intuition - Intuition is sometimes referred to as the Sixth Sense" or "gut feeling," and is essentially the opposite of logic and reason. The dictionary defines intuition as, "A thing one knows from instinctive feeling rather than conscious reasoning." I could add that intuition can be hard to define and even more difficult to quantify because it is not necessarily grounded in facts, but in the subconscious. Based on your experience, your intuition might tell you to distrust someone, but it won't provide you with any objective reasons for doing so. In addition, intuition isn't something that can be learned in a classroom, and intuition is a less reliable tool than logic and reason for analyzing potential problems, situations and relationships because it is so subjective and grounded in the past. Intuition is essentially a hunch based on previous experience, and it may or may not be objective or applicable to your current situation. "Intuition is nothing but the outcome of earlier experience." Albert Einstein

I am not suggesting that intuition has no merit or value because over the years I have met a number of individuals, particularly women, who have a highly cultivated sense of intuition. However, I am saying that of the 4 Elements in your Database, being intuitive dominant is the least objective, predictable and reliable for identifying your needs and defining your problems. From my ministry, I have learned that one's intuition can distort one's perception of reality by giving someone a bad feeling about a good person or a good feeling about a bad person. To examine the credibility of your intuition, ask yourself, *What's wrong with this picture – can I trust my intuition to evaluate this situation or do I need to be more objective and rely more on factual evidence?*

d. Sensory Perception - Empirical knowledge, the fundamental source of all knowledge, is that which we have internalized from our five senses: touch, sight, taste, smell and sound. Empiricism is a school of philosophy that holds to the theory that the only true knowledge comes from sensory experience. I would suggest that one limitation of this philosophy is that it negates the concept of learning through analysis, logic and reason or the metaphysical world of meditation, intuition, prayer or direct religious experience.

Another limitation of having a Worldview that is sensory perception dominant is that our perception is not necessarily reality; i.e. looks can be deceiving. For example, you might date someone you perceive to be physically attractive, and therefore very desirable. However, once you start dating that person you learn that they have always gotten-by on their good looks, but in time you discover that they are very shallow and superficial because they have never cultivated their intellect, curiosity or spirituality. On the other hand, I should mention that one's senses can play an important role in selecting a companion because the way a person looks, how that person feels in your arms, and even how they smell can provide clues for compatibility.

To examine the credibility of your senses, ask yourself, "What's wrong with this picture – have my senses been providing me with an accurate perception of reality, and if not, what is it about this situation that I have been failing to see, hear or feel?" Chapter 4 will improve your sensory perception by providing you with the ideas, skills and exercises necessary to optimize your ability to see, listen and feel what is going on within and around you.

ACTION ITEM #2: Ask the Question – "Everything you want is out there waiting for you to ask." Jules Renard, French author

Have you always given yourself permission to ask for what you wanted or needed? If you are single, have you ever wanted to ask someone for a date, but were too shy to ask? Do you want to know God's Will for your life, but don't feel worthy to ask? Do you want to ask for a salary increase at work, but are too afraid to ask? Do you need help managing your budget, but you are too proud to ask? If you are hesitant to ask for who or what you want or need, you will ultimately have to settle for whom or what you can get.

Now that you have examined and questioned the 4 Elements of your Database of Knowledge & Experience, it's time to begin your Flash Point Experiment by asking God the following question:

What's wrong with this picture?

To ask this question might seem like a deceptively simple exercise to launch your Flash Point Experiment. However, the objective here is not so much to fill immediately your void of peace and fulfillment. Instead, to ask this question creates the longing to know what's wrong, not working or missing in your life that has created this void. To ask God, *What's wrong with this picture?* is to suggest that you truly long for change, your mind is completely open, and without any preconceived ideas about how this question will be answered or where this journey will lead. The picture in question is your Worldview - how you see yourself, as well as how you view your current relationships, circumstances or station in life. The reason for asking this question is, that you can't start meeting your needs or solving your problems if you don't know what's wrong or missing in your life.

As you start asking this question, God will help you to start identifying what it is you have been thinking, believing or doing that has been blocking your path to Peace & Fulfillment. To the degree, you really long to know the answer to this question, to that same degree the question will be answered. "Ask and it shall be given unto you." Matthew 7:7

You will need to be truly fearless when asking these questions, because they have the potential to challenge your personal Worldview and unveil any falsehoods about your life, thoughts and beliefs. When you ask this question with sincerity, it can deliver a very powerful result because it is the first step toward seeking God's Will – the fastest way to get from where you are to where you need to be. When you ask yourself the question, *What's wrong with this picture?* but you don't find the insight and understanding you are looking for, then ask this question of your spouse, closest friends or family. As you well know, your spouse, friends and family can be brutally honest. They won't hesitate to tell you what it is that you are thinking, believing or doing that has caused your life to self-destruct by feeding your ego, going down the wrong path, practicing self-deception or ignoring their real needs. However, this is the very type of objective feedback you are looking for to help you answer this question. Don't shy away from criticism because, if it's accurate, you will be the one it benefits.

If this line of inquiry fails to provide the necessary insights, keep asking God this question until you get an answer. The nature and quality of the answer will be directly proportional to the sincerity and intensity of your inquiry, as well as the credibility of your faith, trust and confidence that God will provide the answer.

Oddly enough, it wasn't until I began my Flash Point Experiment did it dawn on me that if I really wanted or needed something, all I had to do was simply ask. What brought this to my attention was that at that time, I was working for a wealthy entrepreneur. When he hired me, he offered me a base salary and a bonus tied to performance. Unfortunately, the way he had his business structured, I was not getting any bonus money. After struggling financially for six months, I finally worked up the courage to ask him for a raise - not a little raise but a very big raise. I knew he didn't suffer fools gladly so, before I asked him for this raise, I had a backup job in place in case he fired me. We went to lunch together and he asked me what it was I wanted to talk to him about. I told him I needed a $10,000 a year raise and why I needed it. I remember he was eating a salad, and right before he took his next bite, he paused, looked at me for a few seconds, and then said, *Ok, what else do you need?* His response really floored me because I had been needlessly struggling financially but hadn't given myself permission to ask for what I needed.

When you have done all you know to do, but your logic and reason or secular beliefs and ideas have failed to provide you with a sustainable measure of Peace & Fulfillment, you still have options. You can temporarily set aside, but not necessarily abandon, that system of logic and reason and those secular ideas, and ask the question, *What's wrong with this picture?* In a similar vein, if your religious faith and beliefs have failed to provide you with a real sense of Peace & Fulfillment, then temporarily set aside, but not necessarily abandon, your faith and religious beliefs, and ask the question, "What's wrong with this picture?" When you ask this question with sincerity, and with the determination to understand what it is you have been missing, thinking, believing and/or doing that is sabotaging your efforts to attain Peace & Fulfillment, you will *always* find the answer. How does one know when they have found the right answer? I've learned that, I will know that I know, when I no longer question.

In order to launch your Flash Point Experiment, ACTION ITEM #2 challenged you to ask God, "What's wrong with this picture?" ACTION ITEM #3 will facilitate your efforts to start getting answers to this question by challenging you to Make the Decision to Live Deliberately.

ACTION ITEM #3: Make the Decision to Live Deliberately - "Recognizing that you are not where you want to be is a starting point to begin changing your life." Deborah Day, cofounder of the Catholic Worker Movement

The next step in launching your experiment is to Make the

Decision to Live Deliberately. In the context of the Flash Point Process, to "Live Deliberately" is to pursue the **Second Theme of Primessentialism,** which is to make the conscious and deliberate effort to petition God to guide you to the path or course of action that will provide the life lessons and experience your need to attain a sense of balance in your life. Without this *balance* your world would be too unsettled and chaotic to establish the purpose, direction and meaning necessary to make your life complete; a life that is not complete will never provide a sustainable measure of Peace & Fulfillment.

Living Deliberately

To Live Deliberately, is the conscious effort to seek guidance from God in order to discover the path or course of action that will provide the life lessons, relationships and experience that are most essential for your personal growth, spiritual development and physical well-being.

Personal Growth, Spiritual Development and Physical Well-Being are critical for having a well-balanced life because they are the resources you will draw upon to meet your needs and solve your problems., At the beginning of this chapter we mentioned that before you can establish your higher needs for purpose, direction and meaning, you must first meet your basic needs for personal growth, spiritual development and physical well-being. I suggest this based loosely on the psychologist Abraham Maslow's theory of "Hierarchy of Needs." This theory states that **"Unless one's basic needs are met..."** (for *personal growth, spiritual development,* and *physical well-being* **"...there will be**

little if any motivation or desire to pursue one's higher needs," (for the *purpose, direction and meaning necessary to make your life complete).* Maslow's words in bold type. If you are not in a fulfilling relationship, underemployed or without dependable transportation, affordable housing or a meaningful spiritual path, your life would be so stressful and out of balance that you would not have the focus or strength of will to pursue your higher needs. As you seek personal growth, spiritual development and physical well-being, your mind becomes clear, and your life becomes stress-free enough to start identifying your needs and defining your problems.

Within weeks, days or even hours after you Make the Decision to Live Deliberately, you will start being drawn to a path that will meet your needs and prepare you for your next life lesson or experience. As you seek this path, your life will become more centered and balanced, and you will become more open to new opportunities and a broader range of experience. Your faith, trust and confidence in God will increase, and you will become more eager for the insight and understanding necessary to recognize your most essential path. To Make the Decision to Live Deliberately is to say that you're prepared to leave no stone unturned, and no thought not entertained in your efforts to answer the question, *What's wrong with this picture?* To understand why a well-balanced life is essential for preparing yourself for your next life lesson, I think it will prove beneficial to explore the concepts of personal growth, spiritual development and physical well-being, and the role each plays in contributing to a fulfilling life.

a. Personal Growth – One way to attain more balance in your life is to pursue Personal Growth. Personal Growth is all about you.

I view Personal Growth as adding to your human capital – an investment in yourself via deliberate self-improvement, self-determination, and self-reliance. The word, "capital," is defined as a medium of exchange in the marketplace, e.g. stocks, money, commodities, real estate, etc. Your "human capital" refers to the skills, knowledge and experience you possess in terms of their value or cost in society. In the words of Stephen Richards in his book, *Think Your Way to Success*, "You are essentially who you create yourself to be and all that occurs in your life is the result of your own making." When I use the phrase "deliberate self-improvement," I mean the intentional, conscious quest to attain a well-balanced life, while simultaneously correcting any counter-productive habits, ideas and beliefs that might be preventing you from attaining this sense of balance.

Personal Growth is about adding to your human capital by peeling away the layers of falsehoods in your life in order to reintroduce you to your True Self. I visualize this concept in my mind's eye as peeling away the layers of an onion. One layer could be the influence of your authority figures, another could be social conventions, another the expectations of others, and yet another layer, your cultural and religious programming, etc. The idea is to keep peeling away the layers of falseness in your life until you have drilled down to your True Self. You can do this by improving your skills and talents, advancing your career and education, learning new problem-solving skills, staying physically and mentality fit, and establishing healthy relationships - all of which will add to your human capital. To the degree that your human capital increases, to that same degree will your life become more balanced and you will have more confidence in, and be more comfortable with, your True Self. The greater your human capital, the more tools and experience you will have for meeting your needs and solving your problems.

I see this deliberate self-improvement as a three-phased effort. The first phase is about multiplication. When you multiply your talents, you gain the confidence to start embracing new ideas which in turn, will expand the information in your Database of Knowledge & Experience. The second phase of this effort is about addition through subtraction. You add to your human capital by subtracting from your life everyone and everything that doesn't support your efforts to Live Deliberately. This could include rejecting the unrealistic demands of your authority figures, church and cultural conditioning, as well as a conscious, deliberate effort to resist conformity and the unrealistic expectations of others. In the words of American Transcendentalist, Henry David Thoreau, "A man is rich in proportion to the number of things he can afford to let alone."

The third phase of Personal Growth is to create a system with which you can track and measure your self-improvement. Just as a plant needs continuous nourishment in order to grow and thrive, your striving for Personal Growth will also need conscious attention and continuous nourishment. The mathematician, Karl Pearson once observed, "Where progress is measured, progress improves." In order to accomplish this, I suggest you create some kind of systematic, ongoing visual process or written program to track your self-improvement, and then measure your progress on a weekly basis.

One "visual process" I have used is to picture in your mind the different facets of your life, e.g. relationships, career, spirituality, emotional maturity, financial stability, health and fitness and intellectual development, as playing pieces on a chessboard with each piece representing one of these facets. You might not make forward progress with every piece every day, but the idea is to create a system or process for tracking your self-improvement. At the end of each week, ask yourself the following questions:

- **Which pieces have I advanced?**
- **How many pieces have made no forward progress?**
- **Which pieces have lost the ground they had gained?**

Another approach I have used for deliberate self-improvement is to read each month one nonfiction book (secular or religious), one fiction book (usually a novel) or biography of a man or woman who has made a difference in the world. When you read something every evening, you will have a broader Worldview at the end of the week than you had at the beginning of the week. In addition to gaining knowledge and broadening your Database of Knowledge & Experience, you will also learn how others have solved problems similar to yours or overcome the challenges you are facing.

A third approach I have used for deliberate self-improvement was modeled after Benjamin Franklin's system for correcting the "errata" in his life (his bad habits). In his autobiography, he revealed how he took a blank journal and created a grid on each page. On the left-hand column of each page, he listed, from top to bottom, his bad habits. At the top of the page, reading from left to right, he wrote the days of the week. At the end of each day, if he had not fallen back into that particular habit, he would put a check mark in that box. If he had fallen back into that habit, he would put an X in the box for that day. He continued this practice for many years until he had check marks in all the boxes.

You could create a similar chart, but instead of listing your bad habits on the left-hand column, make a list of those aspects of your life that could be hampering your Personal Growth. Below are some examples of self-defeating or counter-productive habits and beliefs that have been expressed by our seminar participants:

- I don't like to read and I am not open to new ideas.

- I don't take criticism very well.

- My addiction is more important to me than my personal growth.

- I resist seeking God's Will for my life.

- I am not educated enough to succeed.

- I give too much importance to what other people think of me.

- I have very few interests outside of work.

To facilitate your efforts to address these issues you could create a Plan of Action for overcoming each. If you don't like to travel, set a goal to take one, short day trip out of town each month. Acquiring new problem-solving skills is a major component of Persona Growth. If you need additional problem-solving tools, you could read self-help books or attend classes or seminars to improve your relationships, career, financial situation or spiritual path.

If you don't have many interests outside of work, set a goal to learn a new sport, craft, language or hobby. If your lack of education is holding you back, take some continuing education classes online or at your local junior college or university. If you have little time for your family, dedicate one evening every week as family time, and then plan activities for that time. If your social life is lacking, you could attend church socials, sign up for dance classes or join a public speaking organization like Toastmasters™. In addition, there are dozens of churches, charitable and nonprofit organizations in your community that offer the opportunity to volunteer and work in the service of others. "Man often becomes what he believes himself to be." Mohandas Gandhi, *The Story of my Experiments with Truth*

I have one last suggestion. When you begin your quest for Personal Growth, stand before your mirror each morning, and say aloud, and with much enthusiasm, the following phrase:

I want my life back.

To state this phrase is to say that you are tired of living someone else's version of your life, you want to get back to your True Self, and that you are willing to do whatever it takes to get there. This might entail dropping a relationship, job or religious belief that is not working for you, or embracing a new relationship, job or religious belief. Repeat this phrase every morning for 90 days. As you do, you will start questioning everything you've been led to think or believe. This can be a bit unnerving at first, but as you make progress, you will begin to feel more comfortable with making a deliberate assessment of your Personal Growth.

This assessment requires that you examine closely and critically your thoughts, beliefs and actions in order to determine if you are making consistent, forward progress with your Personal Growth. When your thoughts, beliefs and actions don't reflect your efforts to Live Deliberately, you are not being your True Self because your progress is being checked by self-deception. "Nothing is so difficult as not deceiving oneself." Ludwig Wittgenstein, 20th Century philosopher

Personal Growth helps you to answer the question, *What's wrong with this Picture?* by encouraging you to examine your current circumstances and station in life in order to determine what's missing or not working, and to understand what kinds of unclear thinking or counter-productive habits are preventing you from achieving a meaningful life. In addition, this examination will help you to determine if you are being your True Self or living someone else's version of your life. Personal Growth is critical for establishing a sense of purpose, direction and meaning because when your human capital is high, your goals and aspirations will be high. When you set your standards high you won't allow yourself to settle for just any career, relationship or spiritual path.

With Personal Growth comes the self-improvement, self-reliance, self-education and problem-solving skills necessary to meet your needs. I've learned that, there are no limits to the amount of value I can add to my human capital, other than those I have set for myself.

b. Spiritual Development – The second way to attain a more balanced life is to pursue Spiritual Development. At its most basic, Spiritual Development is about seeking God's Will for your life. When I use the term Spiritual Development, I am not alluding to spiritualism, theology, seances or institutionalized religion. I am talking about a deliberate effort to cultivate and improve your personal relationship with God, living a more righteous life, striving to make a difference in the world and selfless service to others.

I would suggest that this righteous life includes empathy for the human condition. By this I mean, being mindful of, and making some kind of contribution to alleviate, the suffering of the less fortunate in our society, e.g. at-risk populations like the homeless, the illiterate, the poor, infirm, the illiterate, the hungry, the incarcerated, etc. You could do this by giving 10% of your net income to your church or to the many nonprofit organizations who serve these populations. As an alternative to giving money, you could give 10% of your time volunteering for these organizations.

When I write about Spiritual Development, I am not talking about slitting in church. It's been my observation that, for the most part, individuals playing church are more interested in keeping the letter of the law (keeping the commandments, and being mindful of outward appearances) than keeping the spirit of the law (seeking God's Will for their lives and selfless service to others). "…for ye are like unto whited sepulchers, which indeed appear beautiful outward, but are within full of dead men's bones, and of all uncleanness." Matthew 23:27 I would also suggest that Spiritual Development is not necessarily about religious creeds, doctrines and dogmas, although the study and practice of religious truths can be a reasonable starting point for Spiritual Development.

Spiritual Development helps you to answer the question, *What's wrong with this picture?* because it enables you to determine if the life you are living is ego-driven, selfish, isolated and self-centered or if it's about a personal relationship with God and striving to make a difference in the world. Spiritual Development is also critical for establishing a clear sense of purpose and direction for your life because by being in-tune with God's Will, this will enable you to establish a more spiritual purpose and a direction that is in line with his Will. It's only through our individual and collective efforts to make a meaningful difference in the world by selfless service to others that will result in the greater good. Like Personal Growth, Spiritual Development will provide additional tools for meeting your needs and solving your problems; tools like a broader Worldview, guidance from your inner Voice, prayerful insights, etc.

c. Physical Well-Being – The third way to attain a more balanced life is to pursue Physical Well-Being. To seek Physical Well-Being is the deliberate effort to meet your basic, physical needs as well as those of your family, e.g. financial stability, affordable housing, good health, dependable transportation, meaningful work, education (both formal and self-education) and physical fitness. Although it is possible to attain a measure of life balance without having your physical needs met, it will be difficult to sustain if you are stressed-out, in debt, have addiction issues or worried about how these needs are going to be met.

I suggest that one of the most effective ways to meet your physical needs is to set realistic goals and create plans of action for achieving those goals - whether this be a goal to advance your career, know God's Will, improve your community or better provide for your family.

The essence of goal-setting is to first, set a realistic goal. Next, you list all the obstacles that could keep you from attaining that goal. You then make a list of how you are going to overcome each of these obstacles. You then tie your goals to a budget and calendar. And lastly, you review your plan of action every week to see if you are staying on track.

As mentioned, it will be difficult to establish a clear sense of purpose, direction and meaning if your life is out of balance due to confusion, worry and stress over how your physical needs are going to be met. As a family man myself, I know that seeking what is essential for my Physical Well-Being can be challenging when I am worried about getting my bills paid and struggling to provide for my family. However, the irony is that it is only when I stop worrying and struggling, and stay focused on my decision to Live Deliberately, that I begin to see how these physical needs are going to be met. I suggest that the surest way to meet your physical needs is to stop worrying about those needs (a reactive mode of thinking) and start seeking guidance and direction from God (a proactive mode of thinking). "Your Father knoweth what things ye have need of before you ask him." Matthew 6:8.

I am not suggesting that you don't think about your health, housing, transportation career and financial needs because these are legitimate concerns. What I am suggesting is not to *worry* about how you are going to pay those bills and meet those needs because worry is a poor substitute for faith, critical thinking, good planning, budgeting and deliberate action.

In my own life, and in the lives of others, I have never seen a single instance where worry solved a problem or changed a circumstance for the better."

The key is to trust that God will provide a way, while you are simultaneously doing your part to make or allow this to happen. I would suggest that you don't have to overcome all of your shortcomings or be without sin in order to have your physical needs met. All you have to do is to be in the process of *seeking* guidance from God, and as you do, it will be revealed to you how these physical needs will be met. I've learned that, to the degree that I seek God's Will, to that same degree will I have God in my life; and to the degree that I have God in my life, to that same degree will my needs be met.

Keep in mind that the primary goal of Physical Well-Being is to meet your physical needs and the essential, physical needs of your family. The goal is not about fulfilling your worldly wants and desires or feeding your ego. I suggest that any money beyond providing the essentials for your family could go to make a difference in your community, e.g. to local churches, schools, charities and non-profit organizations.

I am not suggesting that a life of extravagant homes, expensive clothes and jewelry, and luxury automobiles is necessarily bad or wrong. However, one concern I have about striving for a luxurious lifestyle is the waste of resources that comes with it. Why own a large, extravagant home when you can only live in one room at a time? Why drive a luxury car when it won't get you from point A to point B any better than an economy car? Why buy a $8,000.00 Rolex watch when a $50.00 Timex watch will provide the same time? Why buy expensive, fashionable clothes when they won't keep you any more comfortable than clothes purchased from a thrift store? The answer to each of these questions is that they are largely about pride, position, social status, vanity, feeding one's ego, fashion, seeking the approval of one's peers or conforming to the expectations of others.

Another concern I have about pursuing riches is the myth that an abundance of money will buy peace, happiness or security. Helen Keller believed that, "Once you realize that security is a myth, you're free." The reality is that money, in and of itself, doesn't create anything nor can it guarantee peace, fulfillment or security. I've learned from experience that money can pay for a wedding, but it can't buy love. Money can buy a book, but not wisdom. Money can buy power and prestige, but not class or character. To further illustrate the limits of what money can't do, I relate the story of a man in Houston, Texas who won $31 million in the Texas Lottery. Immediately after winning the lottery, he bought houses for himself and his extended family, purchased several luxury automobiles and expensive jewelry for his wife, made a number of impulsive investments and gave money gifts to friends and family. Twenty months after winning this money, his wife divorced him, his daughter had become a cocaine addict and he was broke. He checked into a hotel and committed suicide. He left a note for his financial advisor that read, "Winning the lottery was the worst thing that ever happened to me."

Physical Well-Being helps you to answer the question, *What's wrong with this picture?* because it challenges you to determine if you are truly striving to meet your physical needs or simply feeding your ego and justifying your current lifestyle. In addition, when you are in good physical condition, your mind is clear and alert which helps you to better meet your needs and solve your problems. Good physical condition also provides tools to meet those needs and solve those problems, e.g. a more focused mindset, the strength and stamina to work through any problems, the financial means to support yourself and/or family.

Now that you have made the decision to live more deliberately, it is time to establish a value system that will provide you with the criteria necessary to assess accurately your thoughts, beliefs and actions as well as those of others.

ACTION ITEM #4: Utilize the Reality Touchstone – "Reality for some people is broader than it is for others, because they have looked more, lived more, read more and thought more." Thomas A. Harris, *Notes to Myself*

Since it was your thoughts, beliefs and actions that led you to this particular crossroads, this ACTION ITEM will provide you with some proven tools for examining the credibility of those thoughts, beliefs and actions. These tools are crucial for problem-solving because there is a high probability that if you are not experiencing a meaningful life it's because of the way you think, what you believe, and/or how you act. If you need your life experience to change or be different, I would suggest that you need to rethink the credibility of your thoughts, beliefs and actions. The Reality Touchstone will also help you to determine what's missing or not working in your life.

As mentioned earlier, much of what we hold to be real and true comes from the collective ideas, beliefs, values and traditions of our authority figures, religion and culture. Therefore, I refer to this value system as a Traditional Value System. A system that the majority of the individuals within a given culture hold to be right, good and acceptable for assessing the credibility of their thoughts, beliefs and behaviors. A Traditional Value System incorporates a wide range of criteria for assessing your own life experience, as well as that of others. A Traditional Value System requires a judgment by the individual. The majority of this criteria would fall into one or more of the following three categories:

1. **Right or Wrong**
2. **Good or Bad**
3. **Acceptable or Unacceptable**

I have a number of concerns regarding this Traditional Value System. One concern is that everyone thinks his individual beliefs and value system is the *right* system, and anyone who has a different Worldview must be wrong. In the words of Antoine de Saint-Exupery, author of *The Little Prince*, "The need to be right blinds people." This need to be right can block your forward progress when you seek the path you perceive to be right, good or acceptable instead of the path that is most essential for your personal growth, spiritual development and physical well-being. Unfortunately, being right is not enough because what each individual perceives to be right is not necessarily real or true, which is the source of much conflict between nations, religions and individuals.

For me, this Traditional Value System did not provide the assessment criteria necessary to evaluate my life experience or support my efforts to Live Deliberately. I don't know if this was because it was a good system, but I simply didn't apply it well enough or often enough or because I needed to cultivate a more inclusive or at least a different value system. What I did know was that there was something wrong or amiss with this Traditional Value System because I continued to make poor choices and Peace & Fulfillment remained elusive. By the time I began my Flash Point Experiment, I decided to set aside my Traditional Value System of right and wrong, but I didn't abandon it. I then set out to establish a value system that was more inclusive, one with which I could more objectively assess the credibility of my thoughts, beliefs and actions.

After a good bit of study and reflection, I incorporated concepts from the scriptures, Reality Therapy, Pragmatism and Transcendentalism, and came up with an alternate value system. With the scriptures, we have the authority of God embodied in his teachings and the ideal example for moral conduct. From Reality Therapy, we learn the value of meeting one's needs. From Pragmatism, we learn how our thoughts shape our lives. And from Transcendentalism, we learn there are higher sources than logic and reason, and that people are at their very best when truly self-reliant and independent. I refer to this value system as The Reality Touchstone. The Reality Touchstone is not about judgment, but about observation to determine what is real, true and essential. Subsequently, The Reality Touchstone provides the following criteria for assessing one's life, thoughts, beliefs, actions and relationships.

1. **Is it Real?**
2. **Is it True?**
3. **Is it Essential?**

These three questions, *Is it real? Is it true? and Is it essential?* serve as the driving force of Primessentialism - a kind of "Reality Touchstone." To better understand these concepts, I think it will be useful to provide some definitions that are specific to the Flash Point Process.

The Reality Touchstone

Is it real? Is it true? Is it essential?

Before modern times, a touchstone was a dark stone such as fieldstone, slate or lydite that merchants used for assaying precious metal alloys. These merchants rubbed the metal they were testing on the touchstone, and then they rubbed a metal of known purity (gold or silver) on the stone right next to it in order to see how well they matched. The touchstone was the tool by which to test the authenticity and credibility of various metals. For the purposes of the Flash Point Process, these three questions, *Is it real? Is it true? Is it essential?* will serve as a kind of Reality Touchstone to assay the credibility of your thoughts, beliefs and actions. If your Traditional Value System has failed to provide you with the guidance you need, I suggest you make this "Touchstone" the primary tool for assessing your life experience.

Is it real? (tangible, not imagined) – Trying to understand whether or not something is real is the first step toward identifying your needs and defining your problems. The reason for this is that, if you incorrectly identify your needs or poorly define your problems, you could waste a lot of time and energy trying to meet the wrong needs or solve the wrong problems.

Determining what is or is not real can be a challenge because we encounter daily so many distortions of realty. There are reality TV shows that offer a scripted version of life, love and marriage that we are led to believe are real. There are romance novels that depict a fantasy version of love and relationships. And there are movies infused with convoluted scenarios that rarely exist in the real world. It's not my purpose here to lay down a philosophical treatise on the nature of reality. My purpose is to simply introduce some very general categories of reality to help my readers be aware that the concept that we refer to as reality can vary from person to person, based on their individual perceptions of that reality. For this course of instruction, I have divided the concept of reality into the following three, general categories:

- **Objective Reality**
- **Subjective Realities**
- **Fabricated Realities**

I would suggest that **Objective Reality** is the reality that exists outside one's individual perception of reality. It's the way things are regardless of how we think they are or want them to be. It is absolute and unchanging, e.g. other stars exist in the universe even if they are beyond my perception, and regardless of my beliefs or cultural influences, this reality will continue to exist. The earth is round, even if I look out my window and perceive it to be flat. When I use the term "real," I am referring to Objective Reality - the reality that exists independently of our individual perceptions or what any given culture believes it should be. In the words of American author Phillip K. Dick, "Reality is that which, when you stop believing in it, doesn't go away."

A **Subjective Reality** is the reality inside one's own mind. It's each individual's perception of reality. It is subjective because it differs from person to person and can change significantly and frequently over the course of one's lifetime. For example, some of the things you believed strongly to be real at one point in your life might be dismissed outright later in life, e.g. the reality of the Easter Bunny, Santa Clause or the Tooth Fairy. Subjective Reality is unique to each individual - it's how they see things are, but not necessarily how they actually are. Subjective Reality is the most vulnerable to self-deception, consequently, it's what you want to be real, but isn't necessarily real, e.g. your self-image, your beliefs and opinions, your Worldview, etc.

I refer to the third kind of reality as a **Constructed Reality** – a social construct based on the social norms, traditions and expectations of any given culture. It's what any particular culture mandates to be right, good and acceptable, not unlike "The Matrix" in the movie franchise of the same name. This Fabricated Reality or Matrix dictates virtually every facet of our lives from the cradle to the grave. It encompasses everything that any given culture deems to be right, good or acceptable, as well as the "correct" way to think, believe and act. It also includes the socially approved morals and values, the acceptable norms for fashion, social, religious and political conformity, as well as what should constitute a healthy relationship, marriage, success and a meaningful life. The goal of all this cultural conditioning is conformity within the Matrix, to make everyone think, believe and act the same.

Is it true? (valid, universally applicable) – In addition to asking if something is real, a second criterion is to ask if it is true. The reason this is important is because it's possible for something to be real, but not true. This distinction is important because false beliefs about a need, problem or situation can make it difficult to identify or solve. To illustrate, let's say that your marriage or relationship is failing and you believe that the problem lies solely with your companion. However real this seems to you, it does not necessarily mean that this is actually true. To think or believe such could be self-deception, which in turn would prevent you from identifying the issues clearly enough to resolve your problems and salvage that relationship.

I realize that words like *true* and *truth* lend themselves to a wide range of interpretation and they can be very subjective. In the context of Primessentialism, I would define truth as simply,

The way things and people are as opposed to how one thinks they are or might want them to be.

For example, the Law of Gravity. This law is "true" in the sense that everyone who jumps from the top of the same tall building, under the same conditions, will have the same result - regardless of what the majority of people might think or want to believe. In the words of the 16th century philosopher, Giordano Bruno, "Truth does not change because it is or is not believed by the majority of people."

One of the biggest challenges of determining if something is actually true, lies in the fact that so much of what we hold as true comes from our parents, peers, social norms, the media or educational and religious institutions. What makes this a challenge is that these authority figures and institutions have conditioned us not to question their "truths." The point being that we do not always know if what we have learned from these authority figures and institutions is actually true. To paraphrase, author and educator Carol Rzadkiewicz, "People often accept opinion as fact because they do not make the effort to examine either their own thinking or that of other people, especially those individuals seen as authority figures, e.g. parents, teachers, church leaders, government officials, the media, etc."

As you examine the credibility of the ideas, traditions, values and beliefs you have inherited from your authority figures and institutions, make the decision to determine for yourself if what you have been told, and led to believe, is actually true. I am not suggesting you go on a journey to discover the absolute truth underlying the cosmic mysteries of the universe. I am simply suggesting that you seek the truth without any preconceived ideas about what that truth *should* be. I have learned that,

When I am sincere and determined in my search for God's Will, I will always discover truth enough to find my way.

Although it should have been obvious much earlier in my life, it wasn't until I began my Flash Point Experiment that I came to realize not everything I had been told by my authority figures, peers, educational and religious institutions was true. The main advantage of assessing your thoughts, beliefs, actions and relationships in terms of true or false is that a thought, belief, action or relationship that is true will not need defending, justifying or require self-deception.

Is it essential? (critical or necessary) – In addition to real and true, a third criterion for assessing your thoughts, beliefs and actions is to ask, *Is it essential?* As stated earlier, the word "essential" comes from the Latin, *esse*, which means, *"to be."* Within the framework of

Primessentialism, when I use the term, *most essential,"* I am referring to the path, lesson, relationship or course of action that most needs to be experienced at this stage in your life.

I have found that the Reality Touchstone will always provide a more objective assessment of problems, situations and needs than a Traditional Value System. I say this for two reasons. First, what any two individuals or groups consider to be good, right and acceptable can be very subjective and contradictory. Second, because the first test, *Is it real?* - could possibly be challenged, but the second test, *Is it true?* - is more difficult to sidestep. If these two lines of inquiry fail to resolve the issue, then the third test - *Is it essential?* - will always reveal how credible a belief, action, relationship or position is. These three "tests" will enable you to evaluate the credibility and authenticity of any given experience, situation or relationship as well as any thought, belief or action.

In addition, the value of applying the Reality Touchstone, as opposed to relying solely on a Traditional Value System, is that it eliminates any loopholes and it challenges convoluted logic. It also cuts off all your exits. A value system that doesn't rely solely on authority figures, religious dogma, cultural conditioning or social traditions, and doesn't require rationalization, self-justification or self-deception.

SUMMARY

I. ASK THE QUESTION - *What's wrong with this picture; what's missing or not working that's creating this void of Peace & Fulfillment in my life?*

Step1 is about implementing your 90-day **Flash Point Experiment** when you find yourself at a Crossroads of Uncertainty. It introduces the first two themes of Primessentialism, which are to seek first God's Will, in order to recognize the path that will provide the experience necessary to realize the second theme, which is to pursue Personal Growth, Spiritual Development and Physical Well-Being. As you seek these two, your life will become balanced enough to start identifying and meeting your needs, defining and solving your problems, and make you better prepared to establish a sense of purpose, direction and meaning.

To ask God, "What's wrong with this picture?" is to acknowledge that there is something missing or not working in your life and launches your Flash Point Experiment. With this acknowledgement comes the longing to fill-in any gaps in your lifestyle or personality that are blocking your efforts to Live Deliberately, e.g. education, relationship, finances, career, spiritual path, physical fitness, etc. When you "Ask the Question" honestly and sincerely, you will begin to see clearly what is missing or not working in your life, and start seeing what you have been thinking, believing or doing that has led you to this particular crossroads.

The "How" question we asked at the beginning of this chapter was, *How do I begin the journey that will take me from where I am, standing at The Crossroads of Uncertainty, to where I need to be, on the path to Peace & Fulfillment?* The answer is that you begin by simply, but sincerely asking God, *What's wrong with this picture?* To the degree you really want to know, to this same degree will the answers be forthcoming.

The most important lesson I have learned from implementing Step 1, is that the answer to every problem is inherent in the problem itself. The more objectively and clearly I can identify my needs and define my problems the more self-evident the solutions. I have learned from our seminar participants that many individuals are hesitant to "Ask the Question." I think the primary reason for this hesitancy is that, in their hearts, they know that it was their thoughts, beliefs and/or actions that led them to this particular crossroads. Unfortunately, they often cling to a position, ideology or belief system that is unreal, untrue and nonessential either due to fear of acknowledging their shortcomings, fear of the unknown or fear of actually seeking God's Will for their lives.

Now that you have Asked the Question, made the decision to Live Deliberately and been introduced to the Reality Touchstone, you are ready for the next step. Step 2 will facilitate your efforts to begin filling the void in your life, and make your life more complete by helping you to establish a sense of PURPOSE. It will also provide the ACTION ITEMS necessary to cultivate a more credible perception of reality. This in turn, will enable you to better identify what you need from your career, relationships and spiritual path, recognize the path that will provide that experience, and see clearly any roadblocks that could be sidetracking your Flash Point Experiment.

Baxter Castro Coffee

Step #2: Make the Commitment

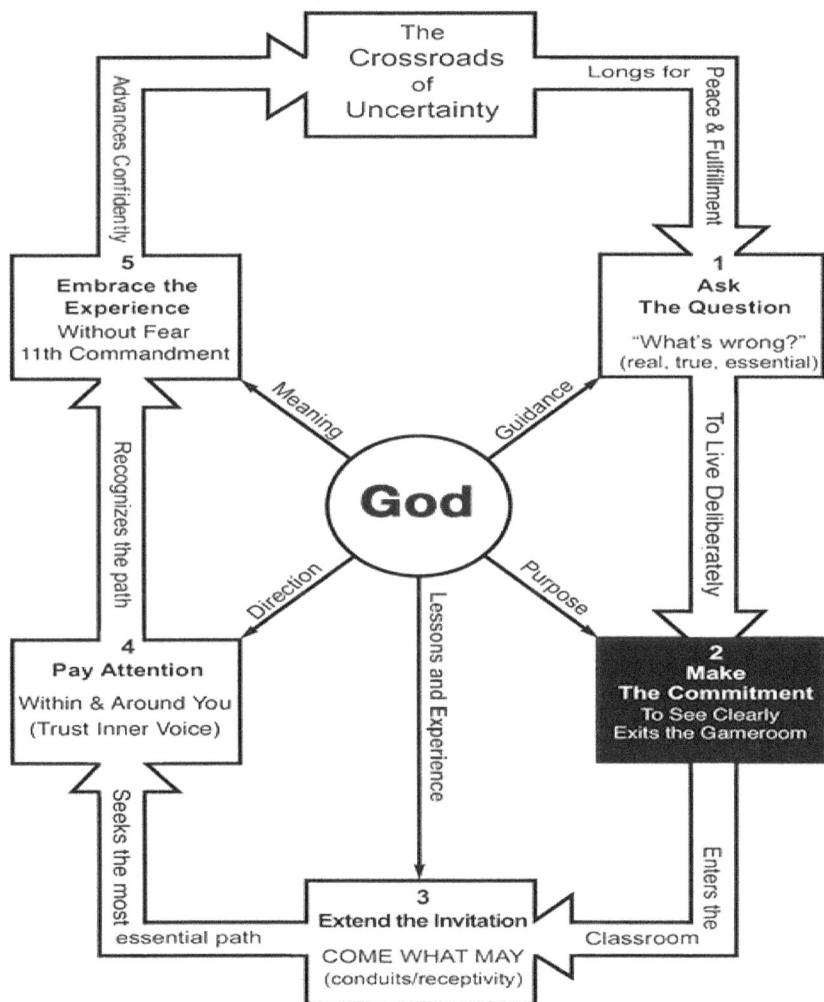

The
Crossroads
of
Uncertainty

Longs for

Advances Confidently

Peace & Fulfillment

5
Embrace the
Experience
Without Fear
11th Commandment

1
Ask
The Question
"What's wrong?"
(real, true, essential)

Meaning

Guidance

God

Recognizes the path

To Live Deliberately

4
Pay Attention
Within & Around You
(Trust Inner Voice)

Direction

Purpose

2
Make
The Commitment
To See Clearly
Exits the Gameroom

Seeks the most

Lessons and Experience

Enters the

3
Extend the Invitation
COME WHAT MAY
(conduits/receptivity)

essential path

Classroom

81

Chapter 2

Step Two: Make the Commitment

MAKE THE COMMITMENT - *Make the Commitment to See Clearly - to see things as they really are, instead of how you think they are or might want them to be.* When you make this commitment, it changes your perception of reality, enrolls you as a student in God's Classroom without Walls, and takes your life off Automatic Pilot. This Classroom will provide the lessons, relationships and experience necessary to attain personal growth, spiritual development and physical well-being.

"Once you have defined your purpose, everything and everyone you encounter is either going to move you toward or away from the fulfillment of that purpose." Arnold Patent, *You Can Have It All*

A. WHY MAKE THE COMMITMENT?

- Because the inability to see clearly will hamper your efforts to recognize the path that will provide the life lessons and experience necessary to meet your basic need for personal growth, spiritual development and physical well-being.

- Perhaps the perception of reality you inherited from your family, or internalized from your culture or religion, has not provided you with the clarity of vision necessary to establish a sense of purpose. Without a sense of purpose, you will be mindlessly coasting through life on Automatic Pilot.

- In addition, you might be at a point in life where you are weary of playing The Game of Life. This could be because you feel like you are losing this game, or you see yourself as winning this game, but still find yourself without a sustainable measure of peace and fulfillment.

- Because you might have spent much of your life trying in vain to fulfill the expectations of others. As a result, you find yourself repeatedly making the same mistakes, and back at the Crossroads of Uncertainty. I refer to this repetitive cycle as The Cycle of Discontent.

When you make the Commitment to See Clearly, you're acknowledging that you are ready to do anything and everything in your power to break this Cycle. You are at the point where you are ready to see clearly what's missing or not working in your life, and see more clearly any obstacles or roadblocks that might be hampering your Flash

Point Experiment.

B. MY EXPERIENCE – As a result of my Great Train Wreck (See Chapter 3), I found myself at a Crossroads of Uncertainty without a clear vision of what to do next. My solution at that time was to settle for the first career, spiritual and relationship paths that presented itself. Solutions that were dictated primarily by my ambition or my wants and desires, with virtually no consideration for the kind of career, spiritual path or relationship that God knew I needed. Unfortunately, 5 years later I once again found myself back at that same crossroads – discontented, disillusioned and frustrated with The Game of Life.

I realized that if I were going to break this Cycle of Discontent, I was going to have to make some significant changes in my life. At first, I tried to change things by changing my external world, e.g. I changed my career, my circle of friends, political party and even my religion. Unfortunately, all of these external changes failed to provide me with any measure of Peace & Fulfillment. At that point I decided there might also need to be some changes in my internal world; the thoughts, beliefs and ideas of my Worldview.

I had always viewed life from the perspective of others (authority figures, peers and church), but this perspective had ultimately failed to provide me with a solid sense of purpose, direction or meaning. In order to attain a more Credible Worldview, I made a commitment to try and see life, relationships and myself, if not perfectly, then at least more clearly.

With my Great Train Wreck came the nagging sense that I had become a loser in The Game of Life. This wasn't so much that I considered myself a total loser, but by that point, I had lost so much in my life that it was difficult not to see myself as such. I decided that I needed to find a way to win at this game, determine what obstacles were causing me to lose at this game or stop playing the game altogether. At that point, I decided to re-examine why I had bought-in to this game, and started looking for alternate ways of perceiving and experiencing differently life, career, relationships and my spiritual path.

The "How?" question I needed to answer was, *Since my existing perception of reality has not helped me to see clearly who or what next needs to be in my life, how do I go about changing this perception?*

MAIN IDEAS – In Chapter 1 we talked about rethinking your perception of reality (your Worldview). We began this process by encouraging your to examine the 4 Elements of your Database of Knowledge & Experience. Step 2 is primarily about establishing a sense of PURPOSE and adopting a more credible perception of reality. A sense of purpose will provide the motivation to make the necessary changes in your life, and will be the driving force behind your Flash Point Experiment.

A more credible perception of reality will enable you to better define your problems, identify your needs, see more clearly any obstacles that might be blocking your forward progress, and help you recognize your next or most essential path.

In addition, a more accurate Worldview will enable you to see what games you might be playing with God, yourself and others. An accurate perception of reality will provide you with a Worldview that is independent from the influence of your authority figures, educational and religious institutions, cultural conditioning and the unrealistic expectations of others. And most importantly, an accurate perception of reality is essential for seeing clearly what's not working or missing in your life, as well as what you have been thinking, believing or doing that has been blocking your efforts to attain peace and fulfillment.

As with any journey into the unknown, your Flash Point Experiment will provide new things to see and different relationships to experience. In order to benefit from these new experiences and relationships, it will be necessary to Make the Commitment to See Clearly. To See Clearly is to see these experiences and relationships as they really are, without any preconceived ideas or illusions about how they should be. This Commitment to See Clearly will reveal a more Credible Worldview, and enroll you in God's Classroom without Walls. This classroom will provide you with the life lessons and relationship experience necessary to attain personal growth, spiritual development and physical well-being. See ACTION ITEM #2 for more on this classroom.

The **Third Theme of Primessentialism** is to establish a sense of purpose, direction and meaning - the three pre-requisites needed to make your life complete. This chapter will begin by helping you to determine the first part of this theme, which is to establish a sense of PURPOSE. Chapter 4 will provide the navigational tools necessary to determine a sense of DIRECTION, and Chapter 5, the insight to establish a sense of

MEANING.

Establishing a sense of PURPOSE is the 1st Prerequisite for making your life complete. As you prepare for your journey through life and relationships, it will first be necessary to establish a sense of purpose so you will have a well-defined reason for making this journey. Without a sense of purpose, you won't have the strength of will or determination to stay on course when you are confronted with challenges, problems or roadblocks on your journey.

Establishing a Sense of Purpose

Over the past 20 years, I have taught the Flash Point Process to hundreds of individuals. From this experience, I have witnessed first-hand the tragedy of men and women whose lives had no clearly defined sense of purpose. I have learned that, the primary reason so many individuals have never established a sense of purpose is because they have been living someone else's version of their life. Consequently, they have never felt the need to establish their own sense of purpose since they were always trying to live up to the expectations of others. Without a sense of purpose, you won't know what your life is about; you won't be living, you will just be existing and coasting through life on Automatic Pilot (See ACTION ITEM #4). If you don't have a sense of purpose, how will you know what needs you have that need to be met? Establishing a sense of purpose will provide you with the foundation you need to overcome any obstacles and work through or around any roadblocks on your path. As the German philosopher, Friedrich Nietzsche famously said, "He who has a why to live can bear almost any how."

It is a basic premise of Primessentialism that everyone needs a "why to live;" a purpose for their life. And yet, as mentioned earlier, national polls reveal that 86% of Americans have yet to discover or establish this purpose. Of this majority, many have never given it much thought, and still others mistake their career, goals or hopes and dreams for their purpose. Because so many of our seminar participants have acknowledged this lack of purpose in their lives, I think it will prove beneficial to explore this concept at length. "The two most important days of your life are the day you were born, and the day you find out why." Mark Twain

Dave Davlin, in the April 14, 2014 edition of the *San Antonio Express-News,* had the following to say regarding purpose, "In my early years as a motivational speaker, I was convinced that the dreams and goals we set for ourselves determine our purpose. On the contrary, through time and experience I have come to believe just the opposite. I believe it all begins with finding your sense of purpose, and that will lead you to your goals and dreams."

In other words, a laundry list of goals, hopes and dreams is not specific enough to provide a sense of purpose. If you make your goals, hopes and dreams your purpose, and these fail to materialize, then your life will be without purpose. If you make your career your purpose in life, when that career is over, your life will be without purpose. If you make the raising of your children your purpose in life, when your nest is empty you will be without purpose. When I write about purpose, I am not talking about an immediate or short term goal that focuses on only one part of your life, e.g. buying a car, graduating from college, getting married or choosing a career. I am talking about a long-term, big picture purpose that incorporates every aspect of your life; what your life is all about. When you have a clear sense of purpose, you have a solid reason to keep going when life throws challenges or roadblocks in your path. What you are looking for is an all-encompassing umbrella concept - a far-reaching purpose that is broad enough that under which all your goals, hopes and dreams will fit, and yet grounded enough in reality to build your life around it.

When I first began my Flash Point Experiment, I had yet to discover my purpose in life. Consequently, I adopted a temporary, all-encompassing purpose until I could discover my true purpose. Based on this personal experience, I would be *very* hesitant to tell my readers what their purpose in life should be. Nonetheless, since so many of our seminar participants have struggled with establishing this "umbrella concept" for themselves, I suggest to them that, *until* they discover their own sense of purpose, they begin by adopting the following, all-encompassing purpose. A purpose they can always change later in life to something more personal and specific:

My purpose in life is to become all that God knows I am capable of being.

In theory, this particular purpose might seem fairly simple, and straightforward, but in practice it can be quite a challenge. What makes this purpose a challenge is that, in general, society isn't particularly interested in whether or not you believe in God or become all you are capable of being. Society is primarily interested in conformity and consumerism, and to this end it strives to shape and mold you into who and what it expects you to be.

I say this because there is so much within our culture that is pushing back against this purpose. This pushback comes in the form of family expectations, peer pressure, religious institutions, social conventions, cultural conditioning and popular opinion, all of which are pressuring you to conform - to think, believe and act like everyone else in the Matrix.

One reason I suggest this particular purpose is, that it is universal and can apply to any believer. Another reason is, that every aspect of personal growth, spiritual development and physical well-being will fit under this all-encompassing purpose. When your purpose in life is to become all that God knows you are capable of being, your every thought, belief and action will direct you toward the path(s) that will provide the lessons, ideas and experience necessary to fulfill this purpose. This quest will provide the lessons, opportunities and relationships necessary to experience a rewarding and fulfilling life.

We mentioned earlier that the quickest and surest way to discover your most essential path was to seek first God's Will – a Spiritual Quest. This Quest will provide the life experiences, opportunities and confidence necessary to become all that God knows you are capable of being. In the words of Abraham Maslow from his book, *Toward a Psychology of Being,* "What a man can be he must be. The desire to become more and more what one is, to become everything that one is capable of being."

A Spiritual Quest to Life

We suggest a Spiritual Quest through life as opposed to a rational or secular quest. A "rational quest" is based primarily on fulfilling one's Checklist of Wants & Desires which includes all the things you want as well as the ideal attributes of a rational choice of career, companion or spiritual path would have, so you can find a path that logically fits your lifestyle. A "secular quest" consists of competitive games and is grounded in cultural conditioning - what society and popular opinion think is the best approach to life, re: The Game of Life, The Game of Work, The Dating Game, etc.

I suggest this approach to life and relationships based on Jesus' mandate that we should strive to be perfect. "Be ye therefore perfect as your father in heaven is perfect." Matthew 5:48 I would further suggest that when Jesus says that God is perfect, he means it in the sense that God is all that He is capable of being. There is nothing unreal, untrue or nonessential about His being. I think the reason Jesus gave us this mandate was for us to strive continuously toward perfection by letting go of anyone, anything and everything in our lives that is unreal, untrue or nonessential. I would suggest that, striving for perfection is not about being perfect; it's the striving, not the goal, that is important. I will never write the perfect book, but I continue to strive for this perfection. I will never be the perfect parent, but I continue to strive for this perfection. In the words of Apache Indian chief, Geronimo, "Wisdom and peace come when you start living the life the creator intended for you."

A Spiritual Quest incorporates the Spiritual Development mentioned in Chapter 1 and involves the belief in a Supreme Being, and the guidance and direction one needs to find her most essential path come by faith, trust and confidence in this Being. In addition to seeking God's Will, a true Spiritual Quest requires that you honestly examine your secular and religious thoughts and beliefs to determine if the beliefs, doctrines and creeds to which you adhere are real, true and essential. A Spiritual Quest also requires that you dare to question those secular and religious thoughts and beliefs, and keep your mind open to any, and all possibilities - *regardless* of their origin.

A key premise of Primessentialism is, that you cannot become all you are capable of being without seeking God's Will because without his guidance you might realize all your worldly wants and desires and have a life that is *full*, but without seeking God's Will your life will not be *complete*.

In addition, whether or not you embrace who or what you discover on your journey will require fierce individualism since it will be a true test of your courage, honesty, spirituality and integrity. I mention this because this journey could call into question your current ideas and beliefs, and possibly lead you away from your comfort zone in the Matrix.

Now that you have established a sense of purpose, the remainder of this chapter will provide the skills and ideas necessary to cultivate a more accurate perception of reality, better identify what's missing or not working in your life, and begin fulfilling that purpose by encouraging you to:

- Break from the "herd mentality" (WHAT I'VE LEARNED).
- Question what price you are willing to pay to become all that God knows you are capable of being (THE QUESTION).
- Make the Commitment to See Clearly (ACTION ITEM 1)
- Adopt a more Credible Worldview. (ACTION ITEM #2)

- Identify any roadblocks that might be hampering your forward progress. (ACTION ITEM #3)
- Stop "sleepwalking" through life. ACTION ITEM #4)

D. WHAT I'VE LEARNED - *My perception creates my reality, and the more accurate my perception, the more authentic this reality. The more authentic this reality, the more essential my experience. To change my experience, I will need to change my perception.* "The dissenter is every human being at those moments of his life when he resigns momentarily from the herd and thinks for himself." Archibald MacLeish, American poet

As mentioned earlier, this **2ⁿᵈ Primessential Principle** suggests that one's perception creates their reality. To illustrate how one's perception creates their reality, visualize in your mind's eye two people standing ten feet apart and facing one another. If there was the number 6 painted on the floor in front of one of them, each would have a different perception of that reality. When asked what they saw painted on the floor, one individual would see the number "6," and the other person would see the number "9." Each would be "right," based on their respective perceptions.

This 2ⁿᵈ Primessential Principle further suggests that, in order to experience things differently, you will need to see, think, and believe differently by cultivating a more accurate perception of reality. A perception that isn't shaped by the thoughts, beliefs and opinions of others, and isn't distorted by cultural conditioning or by

conformity within the Matrix.

If your existing Worldview has prevented you from seeing life, yourself and others clearly, this chapter will suggest that you adopt a more Credible Worldview - one that enables you to see what is missing or not working in your life. A more Credible Worldview will also help you to better identify your needs, define your problems and fulfill your purpose. In addition, a clear perception of reality will enable you to not mistake appearance for with reality. For additional insights about how to establish a more Credible Worldview, see ACTION ITEM #2. I've learned that, to try and experience life and relationships with an inaccurate or distorted perception of reality is like breathing bottled air when the sky is available.

You might have met individuals, like myself, who at one time or another tried to change their life experience by changing who or what was in their lives, e.g. they changed partners, changed spouses, changed jobs, changed religions etc. However, in spite of these changes, they remained trapped in The Cycle of Discontent. One reason for this is, that without a change in their perceptions of reality, there is a high probability that they will view their new spouse, job or religion from the same distorted perception of reality as they did their previous spouse, job and religion. As a consequence, they will perpetuate the same negative experience - repeating the Cycle of Discontent. For instance, I once knew a woman who has been married and divorced four times. With each of her marriages, she constantly found fault with her husband. Unfortunately, if she doesn't change her perception of men, but only changes husbands, there is a high probability that she will continue to repeat this same experience – yet another faulty husband.

In Step 1, we challenged you to examine the credibility of the 4 Elements that constitute your Database of Knowledge & Experience which in turn shapes your perception of reality. The majority of this influence was inherited from your authority figures (your family, religious and educational institutions) or internalized from the social conventions and expectations of the masses. I've learned that, when it comes to my perception of reality, how I receive it, is how I will believe it; how I believe it is how I will perceive it; and how I perceive it will ultimately determine how I will experience it. If I want to experience things differently, I will need a different perception of reality.

To illustrate this point - if the parents of one particular race or religion tell their daughter that all other races or religions are inferior - this is how she receives it. This influence from her authority figures will shape her perception of reality - how she believes it (her Worldview). This in turn will shape her attitudes, ideas and beliefs about that race and religion - how she perceives it. This will ultimately determine how she will interact with that race or religion - how she experiences it. Consequently, she might not ever consider dating or marrying someone of a different race or religion, even if that person could best meet her needs.

In addition to this influence from your authority figures, in order to change your perception of reality you will also need to question popular opinion, as well as the social norms and cultural expectations of the group, the majority or the masses. The English poet, Wordsworth, referred to these masses as "The unreflecting herd." Early civilizations cultivated this "herd mentality" for group protection against predators and the elements. After thousands of years, we no longer need group protection from wild animals, and we have pretty much tamed the elements. However, as with most cultures, we have the "herd mentality" deeply engrained in our collective psyche in the belief that, *There is safety in numbers.* This reflects the belief that if the majority hold something to be true, then obviously, it must be true. I would suggest that it is not always obvious and not necessarily true. Perhaps closer to the truth is that, *There is danger in numbers.* I suggest this because the overwhelming majority of our population have no sense of purpose or meaning in their lives, so how safe would it be to accept their perception of reality, much less follow this herd anywhere?

The herd mentality persists in the Matrix in order to shield ourselves, our group, our nation, our political party, our religion, etc., from anyone who thinks, believes or acts differently from the herd. A failure to see or think differently from the herd will leave you with an inaccurate perception of reality - a Worldview that reveals only how the herd wants you to think, believe and act. Every time you start to voice an opinion, shape a thought or take any action, ask yourself, *Is this how I really want to think, believe and act or merely how the herd has conditioned me to think, believe and act?*

Interestingly enough, thinking for one's self doesn't always come easily or naturally because we have been so culturally conditioned to think and act like everyone else in the herd; in the Matrix. There are many reasons for thinking for one's self. First, following the herd has not provided you with a sustainable measure of Peace & Fulfillment. Second, the herd is a proponent of The Game Room and all the competitive games within this Room, e.g. The Game of Life, The Dating Game, The Game of Work, The Blame Game, The Victim Game, etc. You might not have been conscious of the fact that you have been playing these games, but you are now ready to think of ways to find your own path through life. It was said of Confucius, "The Master knew not must or shall."

Every time someone tells you how you *should* think, believe or act or what you *ought to do*, *have to do* or *must do*, I suggest you challenge or question this by going in the opposite direction.

As you do, your faith will not be shaken and your world will not fall apart. Instead the relief and freedom that comes with breaking from the herd, adopting a more accurate Worldview and thinking for yourself, will enable you to see yourself, life and relationships differently and experience a whole new reality.

To begin breaking away from the herd, and cultivating a more accurate perception of reality, you will first need to decide if you are willing to pay the price to make this break, change that perception and begin fulfilling your purpose.

E. The QUESTION - *Am I willing to pay the price in time and effort to become all that God knows I am capable of being?* - "But no price is too high to pay for the privilege of owning yourself." Friedrich Nietzsche

We have learned that one thing that separates true Seekers from Followers is their willingness to do the work necessary to break from the herd; from the Matrix. I say, *work,* because it will take a determined, conscious effort to critically rethink your thoughts, beliefs and behaviors because what you think and believe has been shaped over a lifetime of following others and living up to their expectations. I would suggest that true Seekers fear neither questioning their thoughts, beliefs and actions; paying the price to fulfill their purpose or adopting an alternate Worldview. Seekers tend to be both broad and open minded. Whereas Followers are reluctant to question their thoughts, beliefs and actions, and tend to make excuses and blame others for their current circumstances or station in life. Followers tend to be narrow minded and close minded.

Speaking of "paying the price," when I was in undergraduate school, I had an art professor named Lynnwood Krenick who, when I failed to turn in an assignment and used the excuse that I didn't have enough time, he would ask, "Did you sleep last night?" When I used the excuse that I didn't have enough money to buy the materials necessary to complete a project, he would challenge this excuse by saying, "Do you own a car? Then sell it!" Because I was struggling to work my way through college, I had very little money and not much time for sleep, his remarks initially offended me. However, over time, I realized that Professor Krenick understood the determined effort and sacrifice it takes to succeed as a professional artist. He was simply challenging me to pay the price in time and effort to attain the level of professionalism I sought for my career.

When it comes to paying the price, some individuals will have to pay a heavy price because their minds are closed and/or they are not receptive to change. Therefore, God will provide them with a series of lessons and experiences that will continue to challenge their thoughts, beliefs and actions until these lessons have their full attention. Others will encounter fewer challenges because they are open to new ideas and receptive to God's Will. A small child who is seriously ill may not be receptive to the bad-tasting medicine or want the painful treatment needed to cure his illness. However, in spite of what he wants or desires, taking this medicine or undergoing that treatment is the experience that's most essential for stopping his pain and making him whole again. In order to recover from his illness, the child and her parents must exercise faith that his physician knows what he needs and be willing to experience what's necessary for his well-being - regardless of how painful, difficult or challenging the treatment.

As adults, we too don't always want to "take our medicine." The reality is that, like the child, in order to stop our pain and become all God knows we are capable of being, we too will need to exercise the courage to "take our medicine." This is to say, we will need to be open to change and new directions and experiences, regardless of how painful, difficult or challenging that change and those experiences. We will also need to exercise the faith, trust and confidence that God (the "Great Physician"), knows what is most essential for us to experience – regardless of how painful, difficult or challenging the expereince.

I tell my seminar participants that there is *always* a way to get from where they are to where they need to be. It's simply a matter of what price they are willing to pay, and what effort they are willing to put forth, without self-justifying one's actions or making excuses. To illustrate this point, allow me to share an experience I had during one of my seminars for a class of parolees in the Texas Department of Criminal Justice.

At the beginning of this seminar, one of my students was excitedly telling me about his new job as a welder. After the class started, I told the participants that there is always a way to get from where they are to where they need to be when they are willing to pay the price to get there. As I did, another one of the participants challenged this by saying his case was different. He said he couldn't get work because he didn't have transportation. I ask him if he had a trade and he said, yes, he was a welder. I told him that the Houston economy was booming so it shouldn't be that difficult to get work. Since he didn't have a car, I suggested he hitch a ride with friends and he said he didn't have any. I suggested he take a bus and he said buses don't go near the welding job sites. I then suggested that he get a bicycle, and he let me know that my suggestion was beneath him. In other words, regardless of what I suggested to him, he would defend his reasons and self-justify his excuses. At that point, I turned to the welder I was speaking with at the beginning of class, and I asked him how he gets to work. He said he drove his car. I ask him if he had a car when he first got out of prison and he said no, he hitched a ride with friends from work. I then asked him how he got to his job before he had made any friends at work and he said, "I rode the bus to the closest stop and walked the rest of the way."

My point being, there is *always* a way to become all that God knows you are capable of being if you are willing to pay the price in time and effort to get from where you are to where you need to be. In the words of John Rohn, American author and entrepreneur:

"If it is important to you, you will find a way. If not, you will find an excuse."

F. ACTION ITEMS - "To see clearly is poetry, prophecy and religion, all in one." - John Ruskin, English art critic

Now that you have established the sense of purpose to become all that God knows you are capable of being, and are willing to pay the price to achieve this, the ACTION ITEMS in this chapter will facilitate your efforts to better identify your needs, define your problems and start fulfilling that purpose. It will do this by challenging you to make the Commitment to See Clearly, adopt more Credible Worldview and understand the value of disconnecting your "Automatic Pilot."

Another reason for making this commitment is that the inability to see clearly makes it difficult to recognize your next or most essential path(s). What makes this difficult is that we tend, not to see things as they really are, instead we see:

- **Who and what we *want to see* -** We want to see ourselves as competent human beings, and we don't want to see our failings, self-deceptions, shortcomings or distorted perceptions of reality. We tend to see ourselves, life and others as we want them to be, but not necessarily as they really are.
- **Who and what we *expect to see* –** With a distorted or inaccurate Worldview, we have predetermined expectations about what constitutes a meaningful life, career, relationship and spiritual path. Subsequently, we tend to see only those things that reinforce these expectations and beliefs and we disregard or ignore the rest.

- **Who and what we *have been conditioned to see* -** We have been culturally conditioned by our authority figures, peers and culture to see life and relationships in a certain way. By this I mean that, we have been conditioned to view life through the lens of the Matrix – to see life, ourselves, other people, religions and ethnic groups as our cultural conditioning has led us to believe they should be.

Because there have been so many external influences that have told you how things are or should be, in order to bring about real change in your life, you will need to start seeing things for yourself. Individuals who seek this change aren't interested in playing games with God, themselves or others but long to see and experience life authentically. They fear neither questioning their existing Worldview nor adopting a more Credible Worldview. Their eagerness to learn makes them students of life. With this new perception of reality, they view life, less like a competitive game to be played, and more like a classroom in which they can gain experience and learn about who or what is necessary for identifying their needs, defining their problems and fulfilling their purpose.

Since your existing Worldview has failed to provide the life you have been looking for, perhaps it's time to rethink that Worldview. To accomplish this, you have several options. You can attempt to fix, adjust or modify your existing Worldview or you can simply adopt a more Credible Worldview.

Adopting an entirely new Worldview can be a bit daunting at first, but since your existing Worldview has not provided any sense of purpose, direction or meaning, what do you have to lose? Before you can adopt a new Worldview, it will first be necessary to make a commitment to see clearly. This is necessary because without this commitment, you will be unable to determine if the Worldview you are adopting is providing you with an accurate perception of reality.

ACTION ITEM #1: Make the Commitment to See Clearly – "To see 'what is,' is really quite arduous; one must doubt, ever search, and see the false as false. One gets power to see clearly through the intensity of attention." Krishnamurti, 20th Century Eastern Philosopher

The first step toward attaining a more accurate perception of reality was when you questioned the credibility of the 4 Elements that shaped your Worldview. One reason for questioning the credibility of these elements was to determine if these elements were providing you with a distorted perception of reality. This first ACTION ITEM is another step toward cultivating a more accurate perception of reality. It begins by challenging you to make the Commitment to See Clearly. When you make this commitment, it enrolls you as a student in God's Classroom without Walls; a more Credible Worldview (See ACTION ITEM #2).

To make this commitment requires a relentless determination to see and understand what might be missing, wrong or not working in your life. To make this commitment requires a leap of faith into the abyss without a safety net, and without fear of the unknown. When you are deeply committed to something, you offer no excuses - only results. When the Spanish conquistador, Hernan Cortes, landed in Mexico in

1519, his commission was to defeat the Aztec nation. Immediately after landing in the New World, Cortes ordered his men to burn their ships in order to demonstrate that there would be no turning back until they had fulfilled their commitment.

A Commitment to See Clearly is the conscious effort to see yourself, life and relationships as they really are instead of how you think they are or might want them to be.

There are a number of reasons for making this commitment. First, if you cannot see clearly, you will not be able to recognize the path or course of action that will provide the life lessons, relationships and experience necessary for meeting your needs and solving your problems. Second, you will not be able to identify any obstacles or roadblocks that you or others have created that are hampering your ability to Live Deliberately. Third, if you can't see clearly, you won't be able to see what's not working or what's missing in your life or what you have been thinking, believing or doing that has prevented you from attaining personal growth, spiritual development and physical well-being. In addition, you will start seeing ways to fulfill your purpose. When you make the Commitment to See Clearly, it enrolls you as a student in God's Classroom without Walls (See ACTION ITEM #2).

Another reason for making the Commitment to See Clearly is that very often, problems, circumstances and individuals are not always what they seem. In the words of the American scholar, Ralph Waldo Emerson, "We must learn to separate the facts amidst appearances." When you make the Commitment to See Clearly you will be able to more easily "…separate the facts amidst appearances" which in turn will improve your ability to see through the false and phony in life, yourself and others.

The *facts* that you are trying to see are what's missing, not working or wrong in your life. This is to say, what you have or have not been doing that has been sabotaging your life, and blocking your ability to attain personal growth, spiritual development and physical well-being. I would suggest that *appearances* are a concern because it can be difficult to determine how things and relations really are, just based on appearances. When you have an inaccurate or distorted Worldview it is like viewing life, yourself and others through *rose colored glasses*. The purpose of these glasses is for you to see things as the Matrix wants you to see them. With these glasses you won't be able to see clearly because you will only see yourself, life and others as they have been filtered through those colored lenses.

An exercise I use in my seminars to illustrate how one's Worldview can distort who and what we see, I have all the participants wear 3-D glasses, which have one blue and one red lens. I tell them that the glasses represent their Worldview. I then instruct one side of the class to look only through their red lens and instruct the other side of the class to look only through their blue lens. I then show them a small square of hot pink paper on which is pasted a larger square of neon green and then separately ask each side of the class what colors the squares are. Each side will see a different set of colors.

Next, I ask them to look through both lenses at the same time. When they do, everyone sees yet another set of colors. I then ask them to take off their glasses and look at the squares of colored paper in order to see them as they really are. I then suggest that the red lens could represent how *they* see life; the blue lens could represent how *I* see life.

When we look through both lenses at the same time, it is how *we* see life. However, in order to see people and things as they really are, we will need to take off those colored glasses. My point being,

To see clearly does not mean to see things *my* way, see things *your* way or see things *our* way (our group, nation, culture, peers, religion, etc.), but to see things as they really are.

To make this Commitment to See Clearly enables you to break your Cycle of Discontent because you will start seeing what is missing or not working in your life that is blocking your path to Peace and Fulfillment. When you make this commitment, it alters your perception of reality and creates a Flash Point - the point where you never again see yourself, life or relationships the same way. I can't remember who said it, but as you begin to see things more clearly, it's like grasping an optical illusion. Once you've seen through an optical illusion you can never, not see it again. The corollary being that once you have seen clearly the false thoughts, beliefs and actions in your life and the lives of others, you will never again be able to convince yourself that these things are true.

Making the Commitment to See Clearly is like any personal commitment, you will instantly start thinking about and seeing differently your life, others and your circumstances. It's similar to making a commitment to lose weight. Once you have made this commitment, then every time you think about food, look at food, buy food or eat food you will be more conscious of what you are doing or not doing to fulfill this commitment. The same is true of making the Commitment to See Clearly. Once you have made this commitment you will be more conscious of what you are doing or not doing to fulfill this commitment. When you are committed to seeing clearly, you will find yourself asking such questions as:

- *Is the way I see myself, life and relationships the way they really are or merely how I want them to be?*
- *Why do I keep finding myself at this same crossroads, repeating the Cycle of Discontent?*
- *What is it that I am missing or failing to see?*
- *Am I seeing this relationship, career or spiritual path as it really is or simply how I want it to be?*
- *Is what this person or group telling me to think, believe or act actually true or is it just how they see it?*
- *Who or what do I need to see differently in order to change my circumstances or station in life?*

The Chinese philosopher, Lao Tzu once observed, "The journey of a thousand miles begins with a single step." A Commitment to See Clearly is just such a step. You will be in good company on your journey because throughout history saints, scientists, artists, and philosophers have emphasized the value of seeing clearly. Appendix A will provide some Observations on Seeing Clearly, that will reinforce the value of seeing things as they really are. To the degree this commitment is honest and sincere, to this same degree you will you start seeing things, if not perfectly, then at least more clearly.

ACTION ITEM #2: Adopt a More Credible Worldview -

"Every moment, every interaction, every relationship, every success or failure gives us an opportunity to learn more about who we are and why we're here." Gloria Karpinski, *Where Two Worlds Touch*

Now that you have made the Commitment to See Clearly, the first thing you need to see clearly is the accuracy or distortion of your Worldview. Throughout these pages, we have been talking about how to bring about change in your perception of reality in order to change your life experience. Specifically, we have been discussing how an inaccurate Worldview can hamper your efforts to see what's missing or not working in your life. In Chapter 1, we stated that one way to change your perception of reality was to expand your Database of Knowledge & Experience by adding more knowledge and new information to that Database. ACTION ITEM #2 will add to your base of knowledge by encouraging you to adopt a more Credible Worldview.

Although there are as many ways of viewing life as there are individuals, I have combined all of them into two general categories - a Conventional Worldview and a Credible Worldview. A "Credible Worldview" is an Objective Reality; one that is revealed when you make the Commitment to See Clearly. It exists apart from and outside of the influence of others. It is a perception of reality grounded in Godly truths and made manifest by the universal laws and eternal principles that govern the cosmos and everyone and everything in it. These principles include the laws of physics, moral precepts, health principles, laws of nature, mathematical principles, spiritual truths, financial principles, relationship guidelines, etc. These principles are universal in the sense that they reveal the same reality to everyone, regardless of their situation, secular or religious beliefs or the social norms and conventions of their culture.

Historically, a "Conventional Worldview" is a social construct; a Constructed Reality. As mentioned earlier a Constructed Reality is one that the cultural norms, traditions and social conventions of any given culture has created. As mentioned earlier, this "reality" reflects what the majority of any particular society considers to be *right, good* or *acceptable,* e.g. what is the right way to think, which beliefs are true, which behaviors are good, what dress, social norms, manner and lifestyle are acceptable to assure conformity within the Matrix. The problem with Conventional Worldviews is that they tend to change over time and are not always grounded in reality or truth. At one point in time, the Conventional Worldview held the belief that witches were the cause of natural calamities, immorality the cause of illness, and the earth to be flat and the center of the universe. Even today's Conventional Worldviews have their distortions of reality and truth, and one of the most prevalent misconceptions is, that life is a game. The Conventional Worldview almost universally sees life as a competitive game to be played, with rules to learn in order to win the prize that's wanted or desired.

The Game Room

The dictionary defines a *game* as, "A form of play or sport, especially a competitive one played according to rules and decided by skill, strength or luck." Our culture abounds with game-like phrases such as winners and losers, being competitive, negotiating to win, time out, playing hard ball, getting ahead, you win some/lose some, keeping score, lucky breaks, etc. Virtually every aspect of our society, from the playground to the boardroom, reflects some type of "game." Among others, the games in the Game Room include:

- The Game of Life
- The Dating Game
- The Game of Work
- The Blame Game
- The Worry Game
- The Money Game
- Mind Games
- The Victim Game

All these games have a common denominator, and that is they all offer some kind of "prize" or payoff for perpetuating the game. For example, individuals playing the Blame Game don't accept personal responsibility for their missteps or failures, so they *win* by blaming their failures on others. Another example would be Mind Games. Those who play Mind Games learn the rules and techniques for manipulating others so they can get what they want from them, i.e. to "win" what they want or desire by controlling these individuals. Individuals playing the Game of Life view life as a competition, with their purpose in life being all about winning and getting ahead, In Western culture, this *wining* is about whomever makes the most money, has the highest position, the most attractive companion, the biggest house, the newest car or the most power and possessions to name just a few.

The Game Room requires the participant to determine the *prize* she wants or desires, e.g. the most recognition, the most money, power and material possessions, the greatest earthly or heavenly rewards, etc. Next, she selects the appropriate *arena* or *context* in which to play the game, e.g. the work environment, family group, social setting, church community, etc. She then learns the *rules* required to play the game - the acceptable routines, behaviors, beliefs and social norms. The object of the Game Room is to control as many of life's variables as possible, e.g. power, position, resources and other players. Those who learn to master the variables control the game, and those who control the game determine its outcome. The purpose of the game is to win the prize.

Those individuals who live, work or worship in the Game Room I refer to as Players. These Players strive to perpetuate their chosen game by playing by the rules and striving to convince themselves and others of the reality and truthfulness of the game they are playing. One such example would be the wealthy business tycoon, Ted Turner's justification for his pursuit of wealth by proclaiming that, "Life is a game. Money is how we keep score." I don't personally know Mr. Turner, and I don't know his circumstances. I do know that he has been a generous philanthropist, so there is an obvious benefit to being rich. Because Turner is so successful financially, many individuals have bought into this myth of life being a game. They have never taken the time to decide for themselves if life is in fact a game, and whether or not money should be the measure for keeping score. Although with money frequently comes power, it won't guarantee a happy family or fulfilling relationship, it doesn't solve problems, or assure you a measure of peace or fulfillment. Money only buys things and opportunities it cannot buy peace or fulfillment.

Eric Bern in his best-selling book, *Games People Play*, made the following observation: "Games are passed from generation to generation. The favored game of any individual can be traced back to his parents and grandparents and forward to his children; they in turn, unless there is a successful intervention, will teach them to their grandchildren." In other words, we receive so much positive feedback and reinforcement from our family, peers, and religious institutions for *playing the game* that there is a great deal of incentive to perpetuate the games we play. Therefore, to exit the Game Room requires fierce individualism and the determination necessary to break free from these social conventions, even at the cost of letting go of those relationships, traditions and long-held beliefs that have induced you to play the game.

Since the games we play are derived from our culture, we're not always aware that we are participating in a game. When virtually everyone we know is a Player, then the Fabricated Reality or Matrix in which we live appears to be real or at least normal. Once you have made the commitment to see clearly, you will begin to see these games for what they really are – unreal, untrue and nonessential. I've learned that, *I cannot lose a game I refuse to play.*

One way to Exit the Game Room is to make a shift in your perception of reality - a shift from viewing life as a competition to win (a Conventional Worldview), to viewing life as God's Classroom without Walls in which there are lessons to learn and experience to gain (a more Credible Worldview). Unlike the Game Room, the Classroom is not a game; not a competition, and doesn't require "skill, strength or luck." Instead, it only requires a sincere willingness to have the experiences and learn the lesson(s) God knows you stand in need of.

God's Classroom without Walls

When you make the Commitment to See Clearly, without relying on Players to tell you how things are or *should* be, it opens the eyes of your understanding and enrolls you as a student in God's Classroom without Walls. In this Classroom, there are lessons to learn and these *lessons* come in the form of the people, circumstances and events you encounter on a daily basis.

Being a student in the Classroom has little to do with your station in life (rich or poor, old or young, educated or uneducated, etc.) or with being smart, talented or even a success. However, it has everything to do with the longing to know God's Will for your life, and what you have or have not been thinking, believing or doing that's hampering your efforts to fulfill his Will for your life.

When you are a Player in the game, you are essentially along for the ride, merely a participant in that game. You see life as something that happens to you - what psychologists call an "external locus of control." Players often see themselves as pawns in a cosmic game of good and evil, manipulated by powers beyond their control, e.g. chance, destiny, predestination, temptation, luck, fate, etc. When you view life as a Classroom, you are an active participant in your life. You alone determine which subjects you will study and accept personal responsibility for what and how much you will learn. Psychologists call this an *"internal locus of control."* Students in the Classroom see themselves as being personally responsible for the nature and quality of their lives. Subsequently, they make the conscious effort to learn what's necessary to make their lives complete.

When you make the Commitment to See Clearly, this reveals life as God's Classroom without Walls, and as soon as you start seeing life this way, then every relationship and experience you need becomes your teacher or course of study. Those who seek this experience become students of life, and the subjects in this Classroom include relationships, career, education, spirituality, finance, health, family, recreation and community. Speaking of life being like a Classroom, I've learned that, the individual who won't be taught can't be taught. Individuals who refuse to see themselves, others and the world as they really are, will continue to be Players in the competitive Game of Life, and remain trapped in the Cycle of Discontent.

ACTION ITEM #3: Identify Obstacles and Roadblocks - "An undefined problem has an infinite number of solutions." Robert Humphrey, American Author

Now that you have adopted a more Credible Worldview, you will be better prepared to identify anyone or anything that might be blocking your efforts to fulfilling your purpose. This Worldview will also enable you to see clearly how to identify what's missing in your life and define the nature and source of your problem(s). In addition to the handicaps put in your path by others, some of these roadblocks will be the result of you getting in your own way. For example, you might not be able to find your path, define your problems, identify your needs or fulfill your purpose because you are going in the wrong direction, asking the wrong question, or trying to solve the wrong problem.

In the context of Primessentialsim, a roadblock would be any thought, belief or action that either doesn't support your Flash Point Experiment or is contrary to God's Will. Over the course of my ministry, I have learned that the key to identifying any and all problems will fall into one of more of the five roadblocks listed below. With a Credible Worldview, you will be able to determine which of the following five "roadblocks" is preventing you from seeing clearly what's wrong or not working in your life.

5 Roadblocks to Peace & Fulfillment

1. **You are asking the wrong question.**
2. **You are trying to solve the wrong problem.**
3. **You are going in the wrong direction.**
4. **You don't have enough information.**
5. **You are fighting the wrong fight.**

Roadblock #1: Asking the wrong question. - The French writer, Eugene Ionesco believed that, "It is not the answer that enlightens, but the question." When you can't solve a problem, or find the path you are seeking, it's often the case that you are simply asking the wrong question.

I once spent two years and all of my money trying to get a childcare project funded. During this two-year development period, I had no income, maxed out my credit cards and plunged deeply into debt. At the end of this period, I read an article that ranked industries by ROI (Return on Investment), and near the bottom of the list was the childcare industry with only a 3% ROI margin. Instead of my spending two years asking, *If so many childcare experts like my project, then why can't I get it funded?* The question I should have been asking was, *What kind of ROI would be needed to attract the necessary investors?* I wasted two years of my life, and all of my money, asking the wrong question. Other examples might include the following:

- Instead of asking, "Why can't I ever get a promotion at work?" A more relevant question might be, *Have I really paid the price in time and effort to advance my career?*
- Instead of asking, "Why can't I find a suitable marriage partner?" A more viable question might be, *What do I need to change in order for me to become a more suitable marriage partner?*
- "Instead of telling yourself, I can't get a good job without a college education." Instead ask, *What kinds of opportunities are available for individuals without a college education?"*
- Instead of asking, "Why doesn't God answer my prayers?" You might ask, *Since God already knows what I stand in need of, for what should I be praying?*

In my own life, I have found that when I don't get an answer to a prayer or any given question fairly soon, it often means that I either don't really want to know that answer or I am asking the wrong question.

When you find yourself at a crossroads and not making forward progress, ask yourself this question, "What's wrong with this picture, could I be asking the wrong question?"

Roadblock #2: Trying to solve the wrong problem. - When you find yourself at a crossroads, struggling with a problem that seems to have no apparent solution, it could be that you're trying to solve the wrong problem. Since we all have about the same degree of native intelligence, the challenge of problem solving isn't so much in coming up with the solution to that problem. As mentioned earlier, the challenge lies in correctly identifying or defining accurately the real problem

When I was a college art professor, I struggled to teach my freshman students to draw. Like most of my colleagues, I saw the problem as primarily one of practice, therefore, in theory, the more practice the greater the ability. At the end of a typical semester most of the beginning drawing students could draw somewhat better than when the semester began, however, their work was still very amateurish. After teaching for five years I decided to rethink this approach to drawing, and in the process, it dawned on me that I had been trying to solve the wrong problem. I came to see that the real problem with learning how to draw was not so much a matter of practice, but one of perception - you can't draw what you can't see. My students couldn't draw well because they couldn't see clearly. They could identify an object, e.g. a ball, tree, flower, etc., but they had never really studied it long enough to really see its various features and properties, e.g. its proportion, size, shape, color, etc.

I tried an experiment the following school year. I had two freshmen drawing classes. With the first, I used a traditional approach to drawing, but with the second, I spent the first six weeks of the semester conducting exercises in visual perception. Instead of drawing, we spent those weeks doing visual memory exercises to help the students more effectively see the objects on the table in front of them. By the end of the term, the first semester students who used traditional drawing methods showed typical progress, whereas those who had first practiced the visual memory exercises could, on average, draw as well as second year drawing students.

Today, when I hit this particular roadblock, I've learned that it saves me a great deal of time and stress to stop worrying about the problem and instead, ask God to give me the courage to help me face up to the right problem. I do this because, there have been times when, in my heart, I *knew* I was working on the wrong problem, but didn't have the courage or the will to face the *real* problem. When you cannot readily identify your needs or the nature or source of your problem, ask yourself this question, "What's wrong with this picture; is the reason I can't find a solution because I am trying to solve the wrong problem?"

Roadblock #3: Going in the wrong direction. - When your life ceases to make sense or fails to make forward progress it might not be because you are asking the wrong question or even trying to solve the wrong problem - instead, it might simply be a matter of direction. See Chapter 4 to learn more about attaining s sense of direction.

In my early 30s, I went to work in corporate America. Four years after starting with this large national company, it was split up. The subsequent downsizing meant they were closing my office and I was going to be out of work. I immediately began to panic, and over the next six months began scrambling to find another job. Thirty days before my job was to end, my stress level was going through the ceiling. At that point, a friend suggested that instead of looking for another job, why not consider going into business for myself. Although I had not been thinking in that direction, as soon as I did, all kinds of entrepreneurial possibilities became self-evident. The result of which was me starting my own business. When the path you are on continues to bring delays, disappointments, confusion or uncertainty, ask God this question, "What's wrong with this picture; is my life (marriage, career, spiritual path) going in the wrong direction?"

Roadblock #4: Not enough information. - When life fails to work, it doesn't necessarily mean you are going in the wrong direction; it might just be that you either don't have enough information or the right information to solve your problem or get past your next crossroads in life. To illustrate this point, long before I was married, I knew I wanted to have a family of my own. Unfortunately, I had grown up in a somewhat dysfunctional family, so I lacked the tools and example necessary for fatherhood.

To make up for this lack of information, I identified several men from my church whom I admired as fathers. I asked each one of them why they appeared to have such a great relationship with their children. At first, most were modest and said something to the effect that they were either lucky or just blessed with good kids. I doubted it was simply a matter of luck, so I pressed them a bit by asking them exactly what kinds of things they did for and with their children. When I asked this particular question, I picked up all kinds of great information, e.g. they had monthly father/daughter dates. They set aside one night a week for family night. They did one-on-one adventures together, e.g. fishing, kayaking, going to the movies, field trips to art galleries, museums and other local attractions. In addition, many of these fathers worked on hobbies or home repair projects with their children.

The information I received from these fathers didn't make me a perfect father, but I did achieve my goal to be a better parent than my own father. When you've reached the end of your knowledge and experience, but still can't solve the problem at hand, ask yourself this question, "What's wrong with this picture; do I have enough of or the right information?"

Roadblock #5: Fighting the wrong fight. - When you find yourself at war with the world, others or yourself, the basis for this fight is often the struggle to advance or defend an idea, direction, belief or position that is either invalid, not grounded in reality or is not God's Will.

In my own life, I was once interested in the teachings of a guru in India who claimed to be the "Avatar of the Age" (God in human form). Although I acknowledged that his claim strained credibility, I found the possibility intriguing, as remote as it seemed. This was in spite of my friends and my family criticizing what this man was teaching. After two years of ignoring the criticism surrounding this guru, I went online one day to see if I could learn more about him. What I found were the testimonials of dozens of young men sexually abused by this guru. Although I realized that one or two of these accusations could be disillusioned devotees trying to discredit the guru, I could not ignore the dozens of accusations. I felt betrayed and disillusioned at having spent two years of my life fighting the wrong fight, defending the wrong faith, and fighting for something that was unreal and untrue.

I have since learned to pick my fights wisely. I say "wisely" because there are many things in life that are definitely worth fighting for, e.g. your marriage, your family or home, your beliefs, your country, etc. However, with others, you can waste an enormous amount of time and energy defending something of little value, e.g. you could be fighting to salvage a toxic relationship, pursuing a dead-end career, or defending a position or belief that is unreal or untrue. I've learned that, when my relationship, career, or spiritual path is real, true and essential, it won't need defending. When you find yourself at a crossroads, feeling overwhelmed because your position, cause or beliefs are under siege, ask God the following question, *What's wrong with this picture? Is this cause worth defending or am I fighting the wrong fight?*

I should also mention that for many of the crossroads I have encountered in my life, there has not been just one roadblock to overcome, but two or more simultaneously. For instance, there have been times when I was going in the wrong direction *because* I was trying to solve the wrong problem. Whenever you fail to identify or define a difficult problem or encounter an obstacle that's hindering your efforts to change, the first step toward resolution is to determine which of the 5 Roadblocks are hampering your ability to identify or define that problem and make that change.

ACTION ITEM #4: Disconnect Your "Automatic Pilot - "So often we live our lives on Autopilot, unaware of our choices and behaviors." Tina Hall, actress

Once you have made the Commitment to See Clearly, adopted a more Credible Worldview, and identified any potential roadblocks on your path, the next step is to examine how you are currently steering your way through life, and whether you are doing this consciously or unconsciously. It's been my observation that many individuals are unconsciously sleepwalking through life; while others are consciously steering their life toward the fulfillment of their purpose. To sleepwalk through life is to live your life on Automatic Pilot. I define "Automatic Pilot as, *A way of thinking, believing or acting without conscious engagement - either spiritually, intellectually, physically or emotionally.* When your life is on Autopilot, you are not engaged in the present - you're just automatically repeating what you have done, thought or believed in the past. You go through life without conscious attention or conviction; you are just coasting through life.

To illustrate the concept of Automatic Pilot, think about the times when you have left your job, driven across town to your home, pulled into your driveway and then all of a sudden realize you've just travelled across the city, but you didn't remember any of it because you were not consciously thinking about what you were doing. This would be an example of driving on Automatic Pilot - driving without being consciously engaged in what you are doing. You've been driving for so many years and you've made the commute to work and back so many times, that it's possible to drive past hundreds of buildings, cars and pedestrians without being conscious of what you are doing.

There is a reason why our lives drift into Automatic Pilot. If we didn't do some things automatically (without thinking about them) we would have to be constantly relearning them, e.g. how to use a knife and fork, tie one's shoes, drive a car, swing a golf club, etc. Unfortunately, when we are mindlessly living someone else's version of our life, we are not thinking consciously about where we are, what we are doing, where we are going or why. We can become so complacent from repeating our daily routines, that it becomes easier and easier for us to sleepwalk through life. We are not consciously thinking about or being engaged with the spiritual path we are following, the career we are pursuing, the person to whom we are married, etc. When this happens, marriages, careers and spiritual beliefs have a tendency to die on the vine due to a lack of conscious engagement.

This ability to drive on Autopilot is the result of the complacency that comes from repetition. We repeat what we think, believe and do the very same way every day for so many years that we can do it mindlessly, without consciously thinking about it or being engaged with it.

Doing something automatically without consciously thinking about it reminds me of the story of a woman who was an excellent cook. Over the course of their marriage, her husband noticed that she always cut the ends off a ham before she put it in a baking dish. Thinking this was some secret to cooking the perfect ham, one day he asked her, *Why do you cut the ends off a ham before you put it in the baking dish?* She responded by saying. *I don't know why. It's just the way my mother always did it.* With her curiosity now piqued, she called her mother and asked her how cutting the ends off the ham added to its flavor. Her mother responded, *It doesn't add anything. I had a favorite baking dish, but it was too small for most hams so I always had to cut a little off each end so it would fit in my baking dish.*

Like the woman in this story, you might be going through life repeating the same routines, making the same mistakes or mindlessly adhering to the ideas and beliefs you learned from your authority figures, culture or religion. You do this automatically without consciously thinking about or questioning the reason for, or the validity of, those ideas and beliefs.

With a conscious effort, you can take every aspect of your life off automatic pilot. One way to do this is to start breaking-out of your long-established routines. If you mindlessly drive to work, daydreaming or listening to the radio, you could make more conscious use of this time by turning off that radio and listening to some motivational audio books which could reinforce your Flash Point Experiment. To break out of your routine commute to work or school, you could try taking a different route. If you automatically turn on the television after dinner, try going for a walk instead. Better yet, turn off your television every other evening and instead read a book, learn a new language, study your scriptures or spend a romantic evening with your significant other. You could also break out of your daily routine by pursuing new adventures or pushing yourself out of your comfort zone by taking a personal risk like pursuing a new relationship, investigating a different church, learning a new language, advancing your education, seeking a career move or visiting other cultures. Disconnecting your Autopilot enables you to see things, relationships and your most essential path, if not perfectly, then at least more clearly.

When an airplane pilot wants to take her plane off automatic pilot, she flips a switch and manually takes back control of the airplane.

To take your life off Automatic Pilot, and start seeing things differently, the "switch" you flip is in your mind. It's a conscious decision to try and see things as they really are instead of how you think they are or might want them to be.

SUMMARY

II. MAKE THE COMMITMENT: *Make the Commitment to See Clearly - to see things as they really are as opposed to how you think they are or might want them to be.*

Step 2 introduces the first component of the Third Theme of Primessentialism, which is to establish a sense of PURPOSE (with the other two parts being DIRECTION and MEANING). A sense of purpose is the 1st prerequisite for making your life complete. This 2nd Step is also about changing your perception of reality by making the Commitment to See Clearly. This commitment creates a Flash Point that reveals a more Credible Worldview, one that views life, not as competitive game, but as a course in God's Classroom without Walls. When you make this commitment, it enrolls you as a student in this Classroom. This Worldview enables you to begin seeing clearly what is missing or not working in your life that is perpetuating your Cycle of Discontent. This new Worldview will also help you discover the path(s) that will provide the life lessons, relationships and experiences you need to attain personal growth, spiritual development and physical well-being.

The "How?" question we asked at the beginning of this chapter was, "Since my existing perception of reality has not helped me to see clearly who or what next needs to be in my life, how do I go about changing this perception?" The answer is to Make the Commitment to See Clearly, to see things as they really are instead of how you think they are or want them to be.

The most important lesson I have learned from implementing Step 2 is that my perception creates my reality, and this reality determines the nature and quality of my life and relationship experience. If I want to change my experience, I will need to change my perception. In addition, I must be willing to pay the price in time and effort to make this change - regardless of what ideas, beliefs or relationships I might need to embrace or leave behind. Some of our seminar participants have been hesitant to pay this price because The Matrix (which includes The Game Room) is the only reality they have ever known. They fear that to exit this Matrix would threaten the long-held ideas and beliefs they inherited from their authority figures, culture and religious institutions. In some cases, this will prove to be true, but what they will learn from the Classroom will more than compensate for anything or anyone they will need to leave behind.

Now that you have established a clear sense of PURPOSE, and made the Commitment to See Clearly, Chapter 3 will provide the tools you need to bring quickly into being the life lessons, relationships and experience necessary to attain personal growth, spiritual development and physical well-being, as well as to start meeting your needs fulfilling your purpose.

Step #3: Extend the Invitation

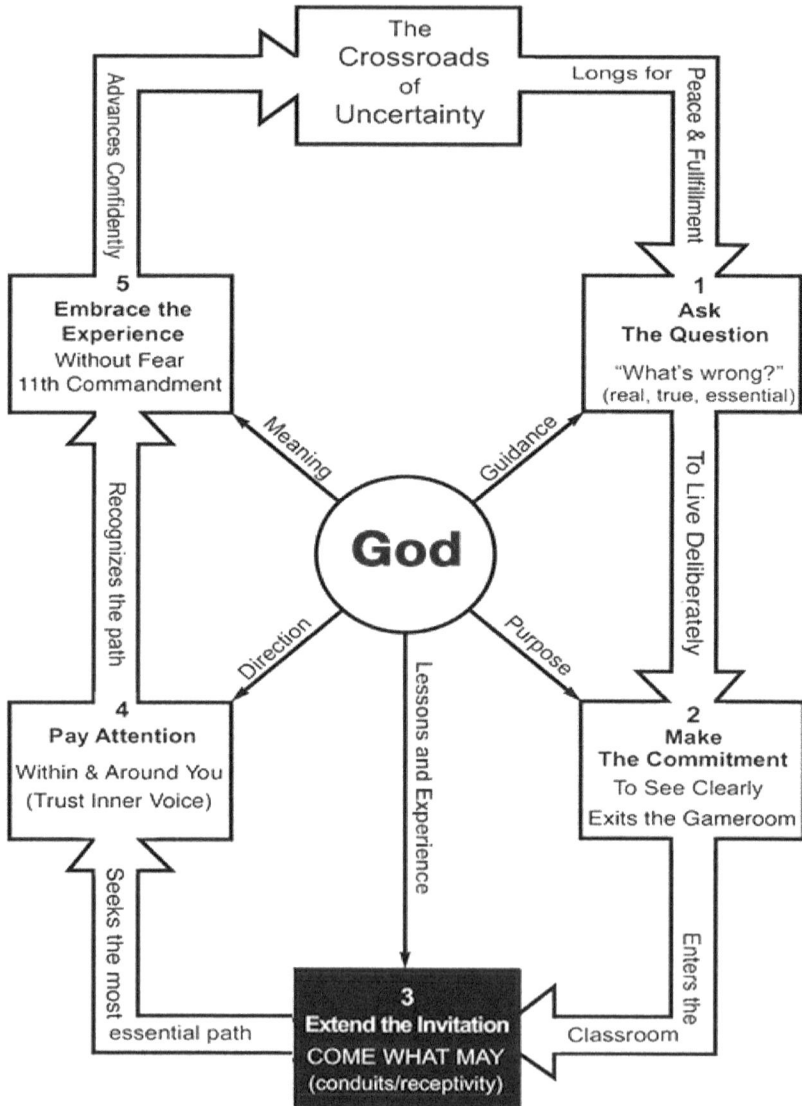

The
Crossroads
of
Uncertainty

Longs for

Advances Confidently

Peace & Fulfillment

5
Embrace the
Experience
Without Fear
11th Commandment

1
Ask
The Question
"What's wrong?"
(real, true, essential)

Meaning

Guidance

Recognizes the path

To Live Deliberately

God

Direction

Purpose

Lessons and Experience

4
Pay Attention
Within & Around You
(Trust Inner Voice)

2
Make
The Commitment
To See Clearly
Exits the Gameroom

Seeks the most

essential path

Enters the

3
Extend the Invitation
COME WHAT MAY
(conduits/receptivity)

Classroom

Chapter 3

Step Three: Extend the Invitation

EXTEND THE INVITATION – *Invite God to send you the life lessons, relationships, tools, ideas and opportunities that are most essential for your personal growth, spiritual development and physical well-being - COME WHAT MAY.* Extending this Invitation brings quickly into being the life lesson or experience from God's Classroom without Walls to which you are most receptive. The amount of preparation you've made and the depth of your receptivity will determine the nature and quality of this experience.

"You can't always get what you want, but if you try sometimes, well, you might find you get what you need." The Rolling Stones, *Let it Bleed*, London records, December 1969

WHY EXTEND THE INVITATION?

- Perhaps you have a pressing problem, circumstance or relationship that is creating a crisis in your life that requires immediate attention. Consequently, you need things to change and you need them to change as quickly as possible.

- You might have tried applying your faith, logic and reason or the strength of your will to solve this crisis, but in spite of your best efforts to *force* things happen, you still find yourself repeating the Cycle of Discontent.

- Because you believed that the things you had acquired, achieved or accumulated would make you happy and provide fulfillment, but these have only left you feeling exhausted, empty and incomplete. This void of peace and fulfillment is often the result of pursuing worldly wants and desires, instead seeking God's Will.

- Because you now have a Credible Worldview, one that will enable you to better identify your needs and define your problems, and you are ready to bring into being the life lessons and experience to start meeting those needs and solving those problems.

When you Extend the Invitation, you're acknowledging that you are truly receptive to the life lessons and experience from God's Classroom without Walls, and you are seeking the skills to make or allow this to happen, regardless of what price you might need to pay. In anticipation of, and preparation for, these lessons, you long to experience a higher or at least a completely different level of life, but you are unclear about how to get there from here.

B. MY EXPERIENCE - Having made the Commitment to See Clearly and armed with a sense of PURPOSE, I felt I was now receptive to whatever lessons, solutions and experience might come from the Classroom without Walls. Because the first year of my Flash Point Experiment had brought the disasters that resulted in my Great Train Wreck (See ACTION ITEM #2), I knew more than ever, that I wanted to get all that drama behind me and get my life back on track. I wanted to get back on a career track, get back my health, get back into the lives of my children, and get back on some kind of spiritual path. I longed for things to be set right, but I didn't want to wait. I wanted all of that to change, and change NOW. In many respects, I felt like I had wasted a good portion of the first four decades of my life, and I was now at a point where I didn't want to waste another day, much less another decade.

Subsequently, I began to try and think of ways that I could accelerate my personal growth, spiritual development and physical well-being. I had been pursuing the life and experience I wanted and desired, as well as striving to meet all the expectations of my family, culture and religion. In addition, I had exercised my faith and the strength of my will, as well as my logic and reason, in order to force things to happen, but without the desired outcome. As much as I hate to admit it, it wasn't until I was physically, emotionally, spiritually and financially bankrupt that I invited God to send me the life lessons and experience I needed to fulfill his Will.

When I say, "to fulfill his Will," I don't mean that I thought there was only one specific career, relationship or spiritual path God wanted me to pursue; there were many possibilities. God's probably not going to tell you where to work, whom to marry or which path to follow, but he can provide the guidance and direction to help you find that path (See Chapter 4 for more on this guidance and direction).

Instead of continuing to pursue the America Dream and my career goals, I decided it was time to stop dreaming, and start thinking realistically about what level I wanted to experience life – what I really expected to get out of life. I simultaneously asked God to show me how to get to that level, regardless of what this might cost me.

At that point, I decided it was time to set aside my personal wants and desires or how I was going to provide for my family. Instead, I started taking God at his word to provide for me if I extended the faith, trust and confidence for him to do so. "…all these things shall be added unto you." Matthew 6:3

The "How?" question I needed to answer was, *How can I bring quickly into being the life lessons, relationships and experiences from the Classroom that are most essential for my meeting my needs, solving my problems and fulfilling my purpose?*

C. The MAIN IDEAS – Steps 1 and 2 were about cultivating a more Credible Worldview, establishing a sense of PURPOSE, and begin identifying your needs and defining your problems. Steps 3-5 will provide the tools, skills and exercises to start meeting those needs, solving those problems and fulfilling your purpose. Step 3 is about time and receptivity - the amount of time it takes to speedily bring into being the life lessons and relationship experience you need from the Classroom without Walls, and the receptivity necessary to facilitate this process.

Regarding the time it takes - if you wanted to spend more time with a friend you could sit around your house, hoping someday he would come visit you. On the other hand, you could greatly accelerate this experience by simply picking up the phone and inviting him to come visit you. In a similar fashion, you could sit around hoping that the life lessons, relationships and experiences that are most essential for meeting your needs will eventually come your way. Alternately, you could greatly accelerate this process by simply inviting God to send these lessons and then being receptive to whomever and whatever comes with this invitation. This invitation accomplishes two things: first, it brings into being the life lessons and experiences you actually need, and second, it brings very quickly into being those lessons and experiences.

In addition to time, Step 3 is also about receptivity. If you are reading this book, you have probably already tried everything in your power to meet your life, career, relationship and spiritual needs, and you are now looking for a better or at least different approach. Unfortunately, many of the individuals who have attended our seminars have not been receptive to some of the lessons, relationships and experience God has been sending them. In order to bring about change in their lives, they have tried in vain to *force* things to happen, This chapter will suggest that in addition to trying to force things to happen, you also strive to *make* or *allow* things to happen by making preparation for, and cultivating the receptivity to, this experience.

There is certainly nothing wrong with working hard, being good or playing by the rules. As long as all that hard work is about meeting your real needs, those rules are self-imposed, being good is not dictated by the judgments of others and that American Dream is *your* dream and not based on the expectations of the Matrix. I mention this because, being good is not enough in itself to guarantee a successful life. I have met individuals in church who are very good people, and strive to keep all the commandments, but then turn very bitter when they aren't successful in their careers, finances or relationships.

One reason people are not receptive to the lessons they need from the Classroom is because they are primarily focused on who or what they want or desire e.g. the perfect companion, worldly success or a life free from responsibility, challenges, conflicts or pain. However, many of the individuals who have attended our seminars have already achieved worldly success and have shared with us that this did not provide a sustainable measure of Peace & Fulfillment. I would suggest that real success isn't necessarily a life free from responsibility, challenges, conflict or pain. Real success is about discovering God's Will for your life, experiencing life on your own terms and charting your own path through life, relationships, career and the spiritual path.

I think it is important to note that the next life lesson or experience that is necessary for meeting your needs could be hurtful, difficult or challenging. On the other hand, it could equally be exciting, interesting or even life changing - depending on your needs, the level of your preparation and the degree of your receptivity. It is *your* lesson and *your* experience; no one else's experience is better, it's simply different. This chapter will:

- Introduce The Receptivity Grid to help you differentiate between your Desires versus your Needs (WHAT I'VE LEARNED).
- Introduce the Hierarchy of Experience to help you determine at what level you want to engage life (The QUESTION).
- Demonstrate the value of dropping your Checklist of Wants & Desires. (ACTION ITEM #1
- Teach you how to bring quickly into being the life lessons and experience you need by Extending the Invitation (ACTION ITEM #2).
- Provide the tools you need to *make* things happen by creating Conduits of Opportunity (ACTION ITME #3)
- Provide ways to allow things to happen by introducing the 4 Keys to Proactive Waiting (ACTION ITEM #4)

D. WHAT I'VE LEARNED - *The depth of my longing creates the void. The degree of my receptivity fills it. To follow my wants and desires only brings into being the experience I deserve; to seek God's Will always bring into being the experience I need to fill this void.* - "Not desiring creates receptivity." OSHO, *Talking Tao*

Is the life you have not the one you wanted or desired? Or perhaps, it *is* the life you wanted and desired, but this life has failed to provide a sustainable measure of Peace & Fulfillment. Desiring a better quality of life is a good thing. Where many people err is in the belief that, if they can fill their void of Peace & Fulfillment through the attainment of their worldly wants and desires, they will be content. This **3rd Primessential Principle** suggests that Peace & Fulfillment come, not by pursuing worldly wants and desires, but by personal preparation and cultivating the receptivity necessary to bring into the being the experience God knows is most essential for meeting one's *real needs*. The more receptive you are to the lessons from God's Classroom without Walls, the more immediate will the solutions to your problems come.

If pursuing your worldly wants and desires can't provide a sustainable measure of peace or fulfillment, how does one go about filling this void? From science, we've learned that a vacuum or void does not exist in nature. Where a vacuum exists, something always comes in to fill it. In a similar vein, when you experience a void of Peace & Fulfillment, you will always find someone or something to fill that void. You might try to fill that emptiness with riches, power, position, the accumulation of material possessions or worldly acclaim. In addition, you might attempt to dull the pain of that void by pursuing a toxic relationship just to have someone, anyone to fill that void in your life. You might also try to eliminate that pain by abusing alcohol, sex, drugs or food – none of which will meet your needs, solve your problems or fulfill your purpose. When you have Peace & Fulfillment, there will be no pain or emptiness - there will be no void left to fill. "People want riches; they need fulfillment." Robert Conklin, author and teacher.

Why differentiate between your worldly wants and desires and your real needs? As alluded to earlier, longing to fulfill worldly wants and desires is often about accomplishing, achieving or accumulating what the Matrix has culturally conditioned you to seek. For example, in not so subtle ways, our culture suggests that success and fulfillment will come once you accumulate a lot of money. The people who have bought into this myth work many long hours, and therefore get exactly what they deserve – worldly success and lot of money. Although a lot of money might meet your financial needs, it won't get you any closer to your True Self, your spouse, children or your Heavenly Father. It won't solve the bulk of your problems and it won't guarantee a sustainable measure of Peace & Fulfillment. It's been said that, *In the café of life, there is no menu from which to pick your experience. You will get served only what you desire.*

Before I began my Flash Point Experiment, my longing to fill my void of Peace & Fulfillment didn't run very deep because I had failed to couple my longing with the degree of preparation and receptivity necessary to fill it. In other words, I longed for fulfillment, but I wasn't prepared for or receptive to some of the more challenging lessons from the Classroom I needed to learn in order to become all that God knew I was capable of being. I didn't want to see myself as I really was or learn about my shortcomings and distorted perception of reality. I didn't want to examine my thoughts, beliefs or actions. I wasn't open to change or criticism, and I was not very teachable. I didn't really want to know God's Will for my life because it had the potential to disrupt my existing lifestyle and threaten my secular or religious beliefs. I had the longing for Peace & Fulfillment, but not a very high level of the receptivity to the lessons from the Classroom necessary to attain it. Subsequently, I gained enough insight to keep me seeking, but I didn't exercise enough faith or receptivity to find the path that was most essential for meeting my needs, which in turn, only perpetuated my Cycle of Discontent.

If you only seek to fulfill you worldly wants and desires, this will ultimately lead to discontent or disillusionment. When you seek the experience that is most essential for meeting your needs, it always leads to Peace & Fulfillment (See Figure #5, The Receptivity Grid").

TFigure #5 The Receptivity Grid

(Reading from top to bottom)

	A.	B	C
What I Have:	√	√	√
What I desire:	X	√	√
What I need:	X	X	√
	————	————	————
	Discontent	**Disillusionment**	**Fulfillment**

Column A - The basis for discontent: When who or what you *have* in your life (√) is neither who nor what you *desire* (X) nor what you really *need* (X) for your personal growth, spiritual development or physical well-being, the consequence is discontent. For example, if what you *hav*e is a worn-out car, but what you *desire* is a luxury sports car, but what you *need* is dependable transportation, you will experience discontent because you don't like what you have, you don't have what you desire, and you don't have what you really need.

Column B - The basis for disillusionment: When, who or what you *have* (√) is in fact who or what you *desire* (√), but still isn't the experience you really *need* (X), the consequence is disillusionment. For example: If the companion you currently *have* is who you truly *desire,* but he or she is not intent on extending their own self to facilitate your efforts to become all you are capable of being, you will experience disillusionment because you still don't have what you *need* - a mutually supportive and empowering relationship.

Column C - The basis for Peace and fulfillment: When, who or what you *have* (√) is also who or what you *desire* (√) *and* it's the experience that God knows you stand in *need* of (√), this always provides Peace & Fulfillment. For example, if the spiritual path you *have* is also one that you truly *desire* and is in fact one you really *need,* then this will contribute to your Peace & Fulfillment because it will facilitate your efforts to meet your needs and help fulfill your purpose.

E. The QUESTION - *What is the level of life experience I seek? -* "Once in a while it really hits people that they don't have to experience the world in the way they have been told to." Alan Keightley, Christian philosopher

This Question is about individual preparedness – at what level are you prepared to engage life? During our seminars, we ask our participants at what level they want to engage life - how they want to "experience the world." This is another way of asking what they want or expect out of life. This might seem like an odd question to ask, but interestingly enough many of our seminar participants have said that they have never given this much thought.

I think the reason for this is that most people are programmed to live the life that is expected of them by their family, peers or religion, without actually seeking God's Will or determining exactly what they need out of life. They accept, without question, the level of life "…they have been told to." This station in life could have been inherited from their authority figures or was assigned to them at birth by race, social and class distinctions or the cultural conditioning coming from the Matrix. Consequently, it has never occurred to these individuals to seek a higher or at least different level of existence, because the unfulfilling level of life they are currently living is the only reality or normal they know. Primessentialism suggests that you will only receive from life what you expect out of life.

In my own life, I have not always sought the level of experience that was most essential for meeting my needs or the needs of my family. By the time I was 37 years old, I was comfortable living the American Dream and was proud of the level of success I had attained. I had an attractive wife and three beautiful children, a home with a swimming pool, two new cars, money in the bank and had just made a profit from the sale of my first business. I had everything I had ever wanted or desired out of life. Yet only two years later, my American Dream had turned into an American Nightmare. I had managed to lose all that I had attained, achieved and accumulated, and my "success" had turned into a disaster (my Great Train Wreck). I couldn't understand how a life that had reached such a high level, could have sunk to such a low level.

It wasn't until my second year of Living Deliberately that I realized my path at the time hadn't been so much wrong, or even a failure, in the sense that it had led me to a major crossroads that had forced me to rethink every aspect of my life. The point being that, my error was not so much that I had pursued the American Dream; the error was that it was not *my* dream. I spent the first 41 years of my life striving to please others by pursuing someone, everyone else's level of success instead of seeking God's Will for my life. In the words of English songwriter, Ed Sheeran, "I can't tell you the key to success, but the key to failure is trying to please everyone." Although there are many levels at which you can engage life, some will prove to be more essential than others, and you will only experience the level you seek, whether this be to fulfill your wants and desires or to meet your real needs – it will be your decision. Although there are numerous levels of life experience, I have listed four of the most common:

Four Levels of Life Experience

1. **The Toxic Experience** - One that is harmful and/or life threatening; one that causes your life to go backward or spiral downward. One that is very detrimental, not only to your personal growth and progression, but also to your health and safety e.g. obsessive gambling, drug or alcohol abuse, criminal activity, toxic relationships, etc.

2. **The Indiscriminate Experience** - One that doesn't move your life forward or backward, you're just *sitting on the fence,* waiting for whomever or whatever life throws at you. An experience that encourages you to "settle" for just whomever or whatever is in your life because you lack the conviction, determination or courage to seek the experience that is most essential for meeting your needs.

3. **The Quasi-Essential Experience** – The word, *quasi* means something that is seemingly or supposedly real and true, but in actuality - isn't. It's about pursuing worldly wants and desires - the things one should experience to attain power, position, possessions, social status or success as dictated by our cultural

conditioning and the expectations of the Matrix, but won't actually meet your real needs, end your uncertainty, provide happiness or Peace & Fulfillment.

4. **The Most Essential Experience** – The experience you need to fulfill your Purpose. One that is necessary to attain personal growth, spiritual development and physical well-being. It's the lesson, relationship or experience you need to become whole or complete, to become all that God knows you are capable of being. This kind of experience allows you to advance confidently on your path to Peace & Fulfillment.

Helen Keller once remarked, "Life is either a grand adventure or nothing at all." On the surface, her remarks might seem a bit naïve. However, what she is saying is that it is only the individual who gives himself permission to choose the level of life he seeks to experience. Creating a new normal is simply a choice. You can choose to view everyday life as either a "grand adventure" or a drudgery to endure ("nothing at all"). If the former is the case, the level of life you experience will be stimulating, interesting and fulfilling. If the latter is the case, the level of life you experience will be one of routine and drudgery, one that is merely an endurance test and a struggle for survival. Thoreau one observed, "In the long run men hit only what they aim at." When deciding at what level you want to engage life, aim high because you will only experience the level you seek.

F. The ACTION ITEMS - "No matter where you are in life…there's always the opportunity to invite miracles into your life." Tania Vascallo, Evolving Magazine, May 2016

Once you decide at what level you want to engage life, the ACTION ITEMS in Step 3 will encourage you to pursue the means by which to get to that level. The experience from the Classroom necessary to start meeting your needs, solving your problems and fulfilling your purpose. These lessons will include your physical health, career, spirituality, education, people skills, finance, etc. because all of these are necessary to attain the life balance your need to make your life complete. This chapter will explore the need for adding considerable depth to your longing for this fulfillment by encouraging you to cultivate the preparation for and receptivity to your next or most essential path.

Many individuals go through life pushing and driving themselves to get who or what they want or desire, only to discover that at the end of their journey they have come full circle and find themselves back at The Crossroads of Uncertainty, repeating the Cycle of Discontent. In order to break this cycle, it will be necessary to drop your Checklist of Wants & Desires and invite God to send you the life lessons, relationships and experience you need from the Classroom. The ACTION ITEMS in this chapter will introduce the tools and exercises you need to *make* things happen and create the receptivity necessary to *allow* things to happen. I've learned that, the time it takes to bring into being the life lessons I need is in direct proportion to the level of my preparation for and receptivity to the experience that's most essential for meeting my real needs.

ACTION ITEM #1: Drop your Checklist of Wants & Desires – "We draw to ourselves what we really want, not what we think we want." Gloria Karpinski, *Where Two Worlds Touch*

Throughout this course of instruction, we have been talking about the value of pursuing your basic and higher needs as opposed to pursuing your wants and desires and worldly success. I don't remember who said it, but *Wants and desires don't bring peace or fulfillment, but only a temporary gratification until the next must-have person or thing comes along.*

I am not suggesting that setting goals or having a checklist are wrong or inappropriate as long as these goals and checklists are supporting your Flash Point Experiment, and not driven by your worldly wants and desires, ego, cultural conditioning or self-deception.

When you are clinging to whom or what is wanted or desired, you won't be free to grab whom or what you really need.

This is often referred to as attachment. Attachment is the obsessive clinging to nonessential material possessions, worldly success, compulsive behaviors, toxic relationships or untrue ideas and beliefs - some or all of which could be preventing you from having a meaningful and fulfilling life. One way to break the grip of attachment is to Drop Your Checklist of Wants & Desires.

What does it mean to Drop Your Checklist? In Step 2, we talked about not viewing life as a competitive game. Individuals playing The Game of Life make every effort to follow the rules established by their particular family, peers, culture or religion in order to win the *prize* they want or desire. In order to make this happen, they begin with a Checklist of Wants and Desires. A checklist that itemizes the idealized attributes or characteristics of their worldly wants or desires so they can win The Game of Life, e.g. the perfect spouse, career, lifestyle, etc.

To illustrate the value of pursuing your needs versus your wants and desires, I share an exchange that took place when I conducted a seminar for single adults in Waco, TX. After the seminar, an attractive young woman named Patty, came up to me and said she was frustrated in her efforts to find the perfect companion. I asked her what ideal attributes she was looking for and she said, "I just want a good looking, young cowboy with a pick-up truck and a home in the country." I told her that individual shouldn't be too hard to find in Texas, and asked her what she had been trying to make this happen. She replied that her she attended area rodeos and fairs, and frequented venues that featured country and western music and patronized online dating sites. I ask her, *What if the man that is most essential for you to experience at this point in your life is not a young cowboy in a pickup truck? What if he is 15 yrs. older than you, and a shoe salesman from Kansas who lives in a city?*

Her initial response was, "No way, I wouldn't even consider such a man." I suggested that since she had tried it *her* way with no success, what would it hurt for her to try and see things differently? I told her that the relationship that was *most* essential for her to experience might not be able to come into her life because her "Checklist" included only good-looking young cowboys with pickup trucks. Since these were the only attributes she was looking for she couldn't or wouldn't see anything else. I suggested to her that the man of her dreams could walk right past her without her recognizing him, because what she *wanted,* was a cowboy in a pickup truck. She agreed to set aside her Checklist of Wants & Desires for 90 days; wipe her mind clear of any preconceived ideas; and invite into her life the relationship that was *most* essential for meeting her need for companionship. She also agreed to be completely open to whomever or whatever she really needed. This could be *no* relationship, *a* relationship or *the* relationship. Sixty days later, I received a call from Patty, and she said she was in love. She told me she had been at a convention in Dallas and had in fact met a salesman who was coincidently 15 years older than her, but lived in a city, and wasn't from Kansas. In the words of the Dalai Lama, "Remember, that sometimes not getting what you want is a wonderful stroke of luck."

Once you have dropped your Checklist of Wants & Desires you can bring quickly into being the life lessons or experience from the Classroom that are most essential for meeting your needs and solving your problems. You can do this by simply inviting God to send you whatever lessons and experience you need – regardless of what this might cost you. I should add that there will be times when who or what you want or desire could also be something or someone you actually need, e.g. you might desire a loving relationship and you might need a loving relationship.

ACTION ITEM #2: Extend the Invitation - "When the student is ready, the teacher appears." Buddhist proverb

Once you have dropped your Checklist of Wants & Desires, you are ready to bring into being the lessons, relationships and experiences from the Classroom that will get you to your next level or stage in life. In order to quickly bring this experience into being, and start *making* things happen, extend the following invitation to God:

The Invitation

Dear God, please send to me all the ideas, relationships, tools, and opportunities that are most essential for my personal growth, spiritual development and physical well-being - COME WHAT MAY.

When I use the word, "ideas," I mean the solutions to your problems. Specifically those ideas you need to start meeting your needs, solving your problems, fulfilling your purpose and making your life more complete. By "relationships," I don't mean just any relationship, but the relationships you need to learn about love, intimacy, spirituality, communication, compromise, loyalty, trust and companionship at this stage in your life. Just keep in mind that all relationships contribute to your Personal Growth, both the pleasant and the not-so-pleasant.

When I use the word, "tools" these are the things that make your life work better and run smoother by improving your Physical Well-Being, e.g. a healthier lifestyle, affordable housing, ongoing education, meaningful work, financial stability, problem-solving skills and dependable transportation. By "opportunities," I mean the opportunity to advance your career, experience a more fulfilling relationship or a more rewarding spiritual path.

By "COME WHAT MAY," I mean to be completely open to whomever or whatever form the lesson, relationship or experience might take, regardless of what lifestyle changes you might need to make, what ideas or beliefs you might need to change or discard, how long it will take or what it might cost you.

I say this because when I extended my first invitation I was so attached to what I wanted or desired, and addicted to how I thought things *should* be, it cost me my family, my job, my health and my religion for God to get my attention. Hopefully you are not as clueless and self-centered as I was, but just the same you will need to be willing to pay the price in time and effort – COME WHAT MAY. It might take a few days, weeks or even months before whom or what you need comes into your life – it will depend on the urgency of the need, the amount of preparation necessary, and the degree of your receptivity.

In addition, this invitation might require some lifestyle adjustments in order to prepare yourself for a new career, spiritual path or relationship. For example, you might need to quit smoking or stop abusing drugs or alcohol before you can find your ideal companion. In addition, you might need to let go of some of your current secular or religious beliefs that could be blocking your objectivity when seeking a new or different career, companion or spiritual path.

When you extend this invitation, don't assume *anything* and don't be addicted to things and relations turning-out like you want them to be or how you think they are supposed to be. When you extend this invitation, I suggest you *fasten your seatbelt* because you don't know how fast or immediate the lessons will come or how life-changing will be the experience. As the adage goes, *Be careful what you ask for because you just might get it.* I would supplement this adage by adding, *And you might get it in a form you were not anticipating.* For instance, you might want to quit smoking, but you keep procrastinating. Subsequently, you invite God to send the lesson or experience that will help you to quit smoking. Soon after extending this invitation, you have a massive heart attack. Obviously, this wouldn't be the experience you wanted or desired, but this experience would definitely get your full attention, and provide the definitive motivation you need to quit smoking. Just bear in mind that when you extend this invitation, the way you want any given need to be met or problem to be solved won't necessarily be the solution you were looking for. However, if your invitation is sincere, it will always be the solution that's most essential for meeting your real needs.

Another example: You might invite God to send you the relationship that is next for you to experience. Soon after extending this invitation you meet and start dating someone who turns out to be very critical of you – pointing out your weaknesses, shortcomings and flaws. Obviously, this wouldn't be the relationship you wanted or desired, but this criticism could turn out to be the very insight you need in order to see yourself more objectively, round-out your personality and better prepare you for your next or most essential relationship. The key to the success of ACTION ITEM #2 is the phrase, COME WHAT MAY.

I cannot emphasize enough the importance of using the phrase, COME WHAT MAY.

When this phrase is expressed with conviction and real intent, it creates a Flash Point; a dynamic of receptivity awareness about who or what next needs to be experienced. Since the objective is to bring quickly into being the lesson, solution or experience you need, the more open, and sincere you are when you say, COME WHAT MAY, the more immediate and completely will your needs be met. When I say, "open and sincere" I mean that you seek the life lesson or experience from the Classroom that is most essential for you to experience at this time, *regardless* of what this might cost you. Sometimes this invitation will bring experiences that are easy and comfortable or they could be challenging and uncomfortable. One more note, when your Extend the Invitation, the response will be on God's time, not your time. It's been my experience that sometimes this invitation will be answered immediately, and at other times it might take weeks, months or years. As mentioned, it depends on three variables:

The urgency of your needs, the amount of your preparation you need to make and the degree of your receptivity.

To illustrate the value of extending this invitation, allow me to share the results of my first invitation - one that led to my Great Train Wreck. At the time of this Train Wreck, I was married and had 3 children. I include this anecdote because lit will demonstrate the value and the consequences of, extending such an invitation to God. I should mention that at that point in my life, I wasn't just unhappy with my marriage, but also disillusioned with my career, spiritual path, health, financial situation, and almost every other aspect of my life. Subsequently, I think this anecdote will be a useful digression because it provides a real-world example of Extending the Invitation.

My Great Train Wreck

In January of 1990, my family and I were living in Mesa, Arizona. At that point, my marriage was in shambles, I was disillusioned with my religious path, and unhappy with my station in life. Consequently, in January of that year, I decided to take a long walk in the desert to reflect on what I needed to do to bring about change in my life. During my walk, a storm began to build, and the thunder and lightning reminded me of the Cecil B. DeMille movie, *The Ten Commandments* with the actor Charlton Heston, as the biblical prophet, Moses, standing on a mountaintop. During my walk, I decided to invite God to send me all the relationships, events, circumstances, tools and ideas that were most essential for meeting my needs regardless of what this might require of me. To extend this invitation I took my cue from Heston's "Moses" and climbed atop a tall rock and challenged the heavens to show me the way – COME WHAT MAY. Fortunately, I wasn't struck by lightning, but neither was there a voice from the heavens – obviously, I was no Moses. I went back home with my existing beliefs intact, doubting that my invitation was likely to be answered.

Later that same month, my maternal grandfather died. He was one of the few relatives with whom I had a close relationship. Two months later the Internal Revenue Service challenged my tax return. Thirty days after clearing things up with the IRS, the company that owned 51% of my new corporation went bankrupt, dashing all hope that I would ever recover the money I had invested, and overnight plunged our family into poverty. Two months later, my wife of 17 years took our children on vacation then telephoned me to say she probably wasn't coming back. To add to this growing nightmare, that summer I had a crippling back injury and three root canals. To compound my stress, all of these events were happening while I was struggling to launch my third business venture. Three months into this new business venture, my wife began divorce proceedings, and as a final blow, 60 days later I filed for bankruptcy. My life had become a complete train wreck.

Although I've never been very patient with whiners and complainers, because of my Great Train Wreck I felt like I either had been hit with an incredible string of bad luck or I was being cursed by God. I had one attorney working to salvage something from my failed business venture, another one working on my bankruptcy, and my personal attorney advising me on the pending divorce. I was experiencing a dark night of the soul. I had hit rock bottom. I was disillusioned, despondent, and overwhelmed with guilt, grief and despair.

One day in late September, I hobbled into my personal attorney's office, limping from my back injury. He told me that even though I probably wouldn't find it amusing, he couldn't help but observe that he had never met anyone quite so much like the Biblical character, Job. He said that he had never met anyone who had lost so much my (health, family, fortune, business, and religion) in so short a time. I told him that he was correct in assuming I wouldn't find his remark amusing.

As I left his office, feeling *very* sorry for myself, I remembered the "invitation" I had extended in the desert back in January. At that point, it dawned on me that perhaps I wasn't being cursed by God or even by a string of bad luck, but was merely getting what I had asked for - COME WHAT MAY. Shortly after this, I decided to extend a second invitation, but this time saying, *Ok God, I am now paying attention, if there's anything left undone, or anything I still need to experience, let's go ahead and get it over with. I don't have much left to lose, so just bring it on. Hit me with whatever it takes to help me change my life, to somehow see the world, others and myself as they really are.*

Frankly, after all I had been through earlier that year, I fully expected that by extending this second invitation the ceiling of my house might come crashing down on me. Remembering my attorney's allusion to Job, I feared I might be struck by some kind of catastrophic disease or other calamity. In actuality, no such disaster hit. Instead, I felt an enormous flood of relief flowing over me like a warm shower. There is an eerie kind of peace, freedom and openness that comes when you have nothing left to lose and everything to gain.

In subsequent years, as I have continued to extend this invitation on a regular basis, it has brought into my life a very rich, rewarding and interesting array of ideas, experiences and relationships, as well as affordable housing, dependable transportation, financial stability and meaningful work. In addition, it has provided the means for meeting my needs and solving my problems. If you are a religious person, the phrase, COME WHAT MAY is the equivalent of saying to God, *Thy will be done-* regardless of the cost. What this cost might be depends on one's individual circumstances. It might cost you your job, a friend, your health, your beliefs – whatever it takes to bring about the changes you need to make to become all that God know you are capable of being.

When the phrase, COME WHAT MAY becomes your daily affirmation it creates a fierce dynamic of receptivity, a deep-seated resolve to experience whomever or whatever is needed at all costs. Sometimes it will only cost you a little, at other times it might cost you a lot. When extending this invitation, keep in mind that it will only provide the life lesson or relationship experience you truly need at this stage of your life. On the other hand, you might get exactly what you want or desire, and subsequently your life becomes a total train wreck. A train wreck because this is what it might take for you to make an honest assessment of your thoughts, beliefs and actions and critically examine your current circumstances or station in life.

The key is to honestly extend this invitation for better or worse, and without expectations about whom or what next needs to be in your life or how long it will take. I mention this because God does not do miracles on demand. Regardless of how dire your situation, problem or circumstances, the Classroom will only send you what you need when God knows you are prepared for and receptive to whomever or whatever it will take to meet that need. To stress the importance of the phrase, "COME WHAT MAY" - you need to be prepared to give up everything you hold dear if this is what it takes to fulfill God's Will for your life. In the Old Testament, Job had absolute faith and confidence in God and was committed to trusting Him, even with his life if God required it. "Though he slay me, yet will I trust him." Job 13:15

After you Extend the Invitation, you can improve your receptivity by keeping an open mind and wiping clean your slate. We suggest that you prepare your mind like a clean slate or dry-erase board. If your mind were a dry-erase board, covered completely in scribbling and writing, there would be no room to write anything new until you first wiped clean that board. In a similar sense, your mind cannot entertain new thoughts or ideas, regarding whom or what needs to be your next lesson, when it is closed or when it is crippled by fear, worry or uncertainty. For a simple exercise to open and clear your mind, see ACTION ITEM #4.

When you make the resolve to be open to any and every possible life lesson, relationship or experience, this resolution won't be deterred, it will not be diminished and will not go unfulfilled. One of the main reasons for extending this invitation is the issue of time. If you want things to change, and change quickly, extending this invitation is a proven tool for making this happen. I've learned that, the more honest and sincere my invitation, the more immediate the response, and the more in-tune I am with God, the more essential that response.

ACTION ITEM #3: Create the Conduits - "For he will reward every man according to his works." Romans 2:6

Once you have invited God to send the life lessons and experience from the Classroom you need, it is time to consider what's necessary for *you* to do in order to facilitate this process. The purpose of ACTION ITEM #3 is to encourage you to do your part while simultaneously being mindful of any limitations of these efforts. I have learned that, although God will prepare the way, it is up to you to find it. I suggest "doing your part" because as a minister, I have repeatedly had members complain to me that God did not answer their prayers or solve their problems. I then ask them what *they* are doing to answer those prayers. I ask this question because many individuals petition God for a solution to a problem, but they would never consider lifting a finger to solve that problem or change their situation. I believe there is a lot of truth in the old Greek saying, "God helps those who help themselves." Once you have invited into your life the next lesson or experience from the Classroom, you will need to do your part to bring this experience into being by creating what I refer to as "Conduits of Opportunity."

A conduit is a channel through which things like water, air or electricity can flow. e.g. a water pipe, an air conditioning duct or an electric cord. When you Create the Conduits, you are making the preparations necessary to allow your needs to be met and the solutions to your problems to flow to you. For instance, let's say that your immediate problem is finding job. From our earlier example, you could sit around wishing and hoping that job will drop into your lap or you could do your part by first inviting God to send the career opportunity you need to provide for your family. In addition, you could do your part by checking the Internet for potential job opportunities, e.g. Indeed, Glass Door, Monstor.com etc., and let your friends, coworkers and relatives know you are looking for employment. These kinds of efforts will create "conduits" or windows of opportunity that will allow that next job to flow in your direction. I think it is important to add that, although God will prepare, the way, it's up to you to find it.

There are essentially two different approaches to *doing your part*. You can simply wait and *allow* things to happen, or you can strive to *make* things happen. The former is about receptivity, and the latter is about preparation. I should add that there is a subtle, but important difference between trying to make things happen and trying to *force* things to happen. The former is about petitioning God to bring about needed change, and the latter is about exercising the strength of your will to force into being the change you want or desire. The remainder of this

ACTION ITEM will introduce some of the limitations of trying to force things to happen versus *making* things happen, and ACTION ITEM #4 will introduce exercises you can implement to *allow* things to happen.

Many of the individuals who have attended our seminars have told us they have tried everything in their power to force things to happen in order to fulfill their Checklist of Wants & Desires. However, their efforts often failed to provide them with either peace or fulfillment. I suggest that one reason for this is that there are limits to what you can accomplish by trying to *force* a desired outcome. Over the years, we have asked our seminar participants to list what they have done to try and force a desired result. The majority of their efforts consistently fall into one or more of the following three categories:

a. **Exercising Their Faith**

b. **Exerting the Strength of Their Will**

c. **Relying on Their Logic & Reason**

I think any one of these three could be a viable tool for creating the necessary Conduits of Opportunity. However, if you have tried these tools and they have failed to produce the desired outcome, the problem might not be the tool itself. It might simply be the limitations of that tool or it could be how you are applying it. For example, you wouldn't have much success trying to hammer a nail with a screwdriver. This is not fault of the screwdriver. The fault is not realizing there are limitations to what this tool can do, and how you're trying to use it. To further illustrate this point, I think it would be useful to examine some of the strengths and limitations of Faith, Force, Logic and Reason as well as how you might be applying them. Limitations these tools might have that are hindering your efforts to create the necessary conduits.

Some Strengths and Limitations of Faith, Force, Logic & Reason

a. Exercising Your Faith: For the most part, I believe that faith precedes the miracle, but often it takes more than faith to bring that miracle into being. It takes real effort on our part. In the words of American religious leader and author, Spencer W. Kimball, "I have the faith to move mountains; give me a shovel."

I have frequently had seminar participants tell me they have lost their faith because they have prayed and prayed for a desired outcome, but without success. I suggest to these individuals that there is a possibility that there might be something important they yet need to learn regarding their faith and how it serves them. Alternately, it might simply be the case of how they are or are not applying their faith. I go on to tell them that faith isn't something one loses, it's something that one is either not applying often enough or well enough. Faith, like love, is part of the human psyche. I say this because everyone has faith in someone or something - whether this be faith in God, faith in one's self or faith in one's secular ideology. When you choose *not* to rely on your faith, this doesn't mean you don't have the capacity to do so. I would suggest it could mean you don't have the will, trust or confidence to do so. "Faith is not a thing one 'loses;' we merely cease to shape our lives by it." French author, George Bernanos

Exercising faith can be very helpful for creating the conduits you need because when you have the faith that something can happen there is a greater possibility that it will happen. I say this because, the greater the faith the greater the confidence, and the greater the confidence the more likely the desired outcome. When you are prepared for and receptive to the lessons from the Classroom without Walls, your self-confidence increases and your confidence will go a long way toward making this happen.

I have often exercised faith to meet my needs, specifically at those times when my path has not been clear or self-evident, but my Inner Voice keeps prompting me in a given direction. However, when I don't have the confidence to follow that path, or my faith is so weak that I don't trust that path, my limited faith hinders my ability to find my way. In other words, my lack of confidence and trust, and not faith itself, were the limiting factors. I have learned that, faith without trust and confidence is merely belief. I might believe that God *can* facilitate my efforts to meet my needs and find my way, but that's not the same as having the trust and confidence that He *will* facilitate these efforts.

There are other limitations regarding faith. When you have the wrong type of faith, your faith is "blind" or it's not grounded in reality. Eric Fromm in his classic book, *The Art of Loving* distinguishes between two types of faith: irrational and rational, with the former being "The acceptance of something as true only because an authority or the majority say so (the submission to irrational authority)." Whereas the latter "Is rooted in an independent conviction based upon one's own rational productive observing and thinking, in spite of the majority's opinion (the quality of certainty and firmness which our convictions have)."

Faith grounded solely on authority is what I refer to as blind faith. By this, I mean that some secular teachers, and many religious cults and institutions, condition their adherents to follow blindly their dogma and teachings and not to question those teachings. This type of irrational, blind faith in authority figures and religious institutions is touted by many as being something of great value. However, if you have blind faith in the teachings of your religion, and your religious leaders have blind faith in the tenants of that religion, it could create a dynamic of what the scriptures refer to as the "…blind leading the blind." Matthew 15:14 Some examples of the destructive outcomes of "blind faith" would be those individuals who believed in, and followed blindly the dogma of Adolf Hitler, David Koresh. Jim Jones, Marshall Applewhite, Luc Jouret, etc. In the words of Einstein, "Blind belief in authority is the greatest enemy of truth."

One last limitation of faith, when trying to force a desired outcome, exists when what you are trying to make happen either isn't God's Will or not grounded in reality or truth, e.g. asking God to help you win the lottery or win back an unsuitable lost love. When this is the case, regardless of how sincere your faith, or dire your situation, that reality is not going to come to fruition.

Faith is a critical component of life because when God reveals a path that leads to your next lesson or experience, at first you know nothing about this lesson, circumstance or individual so you will need to exercise faith that this lesson has come to teach you something essential about life. I have great confidence in, and have the seen the strength and power of faith when it is grounded in reality, and is coupled with confidence and trust. This has been particularly true for those times when I have witnessed individuals petition God to heal their loved ones. In addition, it's been my observation that the right kind of faith can be very reliable, particularly when weighing options where the factual evidence is unclear or not readily apparent. The bottom line is that there are no inherent limitations of faith when trying to create the necessary conduits. Its only limits are those set by the individual, e.g. when one's faith is not grounded in reality or God's Will, when that faith is blind and relies solely on authority figures, or when that faith is not accompanied by confidence and trust in God.

b. Exerting the Strength of Your Will: What I could not resolve through my faith, there have been many occasions when I have exerted the strength of my will to force a desired outcome. Unfortunately, when I looked back at my life, I saw the limitations of trying to force things to work. Each time I tried to control or force a desired outcome I usually did more harm than good, and the cost of using force often outweighed the benefit. Very often, when I resorted to the strength of my will, either I or someone else suffered.

There are occasions when exerting the strength of your will to forcibly create a conduit can be a viable option. This is especially true when you lack the skills to achieve this outcome or you have exhausted every other tool at your disposal. When the chips are down and it's a matter of physical, emotional or financial survival, you can often get past a crisis by exerting the sheer strength of your will. However, to exert the strength of your will to *force* any outcome, will often bring discontent when it is only to pursue something you want or desire instead of something you need. This happens most frequently when pursuing someone or something that stems from feeding your ego, filling your worldly wants and desires, trying to fulfill the expectations of others or when it's not grounded in God's Will.

It's been said that, you will never have to force anything that's truly meant to be. Trying to force something that is not "meant to be" brings only discontent and disillusionment, e.g. trying to force a relationship to work that is doomed to failure, pursuing a dead-end career that's not going anywhere, or forcing yourself to adhere to a religious belief that will never resolve your divine discontent regardless of how much you want your beliefs to be true.

c. Relying on Your Logic & Reason: When I was younger, I thought that logic and reason were the most effective problem-solving tools. I believed this because the scientific method of logical analysis, critical thinking and deductive reasoning is how our educational institutions, as well as most ongoing business training, teach us to think. Just to be clear, I am not even remotely disparaging the role that logic and reason plays in our lives. I have successfully used logic and reason to work through a wide range of problems, as well as to help steer my way through life.

The dictionary defines logic as, "A proper or reasonable way of thinking about or understanding something." The point I wish to make is that logic and reason are viable tools for creating the necessary conduits, but only if one's thinking is "proper or reasonable." Your thinking will be neither proper nor reasonable when it's distorted by an inaccurate Worldview, driven by your wants and desires, clouded by self-deception or distorted by convoluted logic.

Although logic and reason can be very valuable tools when trying to create the most viable conduits, these can't always be trusted to create the best outcome because a logical and reasonable solution is not necessarily the most essential solution. To illustrate, let's use the example of a man trying to force a relationship or marriage to work that is simply not meant to be. This happens when he chooses a marriage partner, not based on love and common interests, but because she appears to be the most logical and reasonable choice since she fulfills all the wants and desires on his Checklist. This checklist might include all the character traits, personality and physical attributes he wants or desires in a companion, e.g. blond hair, blue eyes, socially prominent, nice physique, athletic, etc. However, regardless of how logical a fit she might be, there is a high probability the marriage will fail if the dialog, love, trust, spirituality, intimacy and nurturing he needed were not existing traits of that marriage partner. I would suggest that that God is not going to tell you whom to date or marry because there are many potential partners. On the other hand, when you prayerfully seek his guidance, he can provide feelings of certainty for a good fit or feelings of doubt for a not so good fit.

Logic and reason can analyze and explain many things, but not everything. They can't really grasp the concept of romantic love, God, faith, the power of a symphony, the beauty of nature, the wonder of art or the magic of a kiss. Logic and reason can be very valuable tools for meeting needs and solving problems, just as long as they are not distorted or convoluted, based on self-deception or narrow in scope. In the words of the author of *The Little Prince*, Antoine de Saint-Exupery, "Pure logic is the ruin of the spirit."

ACTION ITEM #4: Cultivate the Receptivity -

"Understanding the need creates the receptivity – which in turn is an invitation for this energy to enter." Daniel Castro, *In That Stillness*

Once you've done all the preparations to *make* things happen, i.e. dropped your checklist, extended the invitation, and created the necessary conduits, it is now time to cultivate the receptivity necessary to *allow* things to happen. To be receptive is to be open and responsive to the ideas, impressions and signals God is sending to help you find your way. In Chapter 1 we suggested that you ask yourself, *Who or what do I truly long for?* We went on to say that when you begin to identify your real needs, the odds of attaining, achieving or attracting who or what's necessary to meet those needs increases significantly.

Understanding the need creates the longing to meet that need, and the greater the longing, the greater the receptivity to bring this into fruition.

Most of what I achieved, accumulated or accomplished in the first 40 years of my life came about because of my efforts to force things to happen with the unfortunate result being my Great Train Wreck. Once I began my Flash Point Experiment, I decided that in addition to doing everything in my power to *make* things happen, I would also start trying to simply *allow* things to happen. In order to accomplish this, and bring quickly into being the lessons and experiences I needed, I tried to think of ways to increase my receptivity to these lessons and experiences by practicing Proactive Waiting.

Proactive Waiting

Proactive Waiting is not about idleness or doing nothing. Daniel Castro, in his book, *In That Stillness,* suggests that when you take a break from busy-ness, from activity, from constantly pushing and driving yourself to achieve, accumulate or fulfill your wants and desires, then waiting isn't that difficult. In that quiet stillness, you will hear the promptings from God and receive the guidance and direction you need to find your way. You won't need to depend solely on your faith, force or logic and reason - it will come in direct proportion to your level of receptivity to the guidance God is providing via your Inner Voice (See Chapter 4).

Although life can be frustrating when things don't go your way, the reality is that you simply might not be prepared for, or receptive to, that life lesson or relationship experience. I should add that seeking your next or most essential experience will often require time and patience. It will only come when you are truly ready, and any attempts to force it to come will end in frustration and discontent. I think it's worth repeating that ultimately, we all get what we need or deserve from the Classroom; the former we get from God and the latter we get from pursuing our wants and desires. Merely wanting something to happen will not bring it into being; you have to work for it by making the appropriate preparations, creating the best conduits and cultivating the necessary receptivity. I've learned that, proactive waiting increases my receptivity to God's Will. To improve your receptivity, apply the "4 Keys to Proactive Waiting."

The 4 Keys to Proactive Waiting:

1st Key: Stay the Course

2nd Key: Be Prepared

3rd Key: Clear Your Mind

4th Key: Allow for Construction

The 1st Key: Stay the Course – There might be times when you're waiting for the next lesson from the Classroom, but you have yet to learn all that's needed from your current situation, e.g. your current career, spiritual path or companion. When your life appears to be stuck, you can increase your receptivity by paying careful attention to whom or what is in front of you in order to see what this person or situation has come to teach you. If you can't or don't want to understand what any given lesson has come to teach you, then you won't be receptive to change and you will continue to be trapped in the Cycle of Discontent.

To illustrate this point, I know a 68-year-old businessman who has been married and divorced five times over the course of 40 years. Each of his wives has been a struggling, financially challenged, single woman with very little formal education and two children. I believe this man married these particular women, not to create a mutual support system, but to create a dependent relationship. A relationship that enabled him to feel superior to his spouse, maintain a high level of control over the relationship and buttress his self-esteem by having "rescued" the single mother. About once every 7 to 8 years, this man gets a divorce, blaming his failed marriage on his then current wife. He next marries yet another struggling, financially challenged woman with two children. I would suggest that everything he needed to learn about love, trust, intimacy and relationships could have come from any one of his marriages. At some point, he will need to take a close look in the mirror in order to realize that his ex-wives might not have caused this Cycle of Discontent. There is a high probability that the reason these marriages failed was because he was neither prepared to work on those relationships nor receptive to learning what's essential to sustain a loving, mutually supportive relationship.

Are you disillusioned with a career, relationship or spiritual path? When you find yourself in this situation, it is only natural to just want to get out of it as soon as possible. However, if you do so prematurely, you could miss some valuable lessons. Stay with that career, relationship or spiritual path until you understand clearly, either why you invited this kind of experience into your life, or what needs you have that are not being met. If you fail to do this, there is a high probability you will remain trapped in the Cycle of Discontent.

When you find yourself at crossroads, continuously getting a different version of the same experience, instead of repeating this Cycle of Discontent, *stay the course*. Stay where you are or stay with whom you are with until you can answer this question, *What's wrong with this picture; why does this kind of situation or relationship keep recurring in my life - what is it that I am failing to see, do or understand?*

The 2ⁿᵈ Key: Be Prepared – In my youth I was a Boy Scout, and this organization has a great motto: "Be Prepared." When you find yourself stuck at a Crossroads, perhaps the problem is not a matter of staying the course, but simply a lack of preparedness. I define a lack of preparedness as wanting someone or something more than your existing capacity to experience it. In other words, you may be receptive to the next lesson from the Classroom, but you are not yet prepared for it.

Just because you really want something or someone does not necessarily mean you are actually ready for this experience when it is a case of needing more preparation. The French chemist, Louis Pasteur, once remarked, "Chance favors the prepared mind." In other words, the better prepared you are for the life lessons and experience coming from God's Classroom without Walls, the more you will learn from these lessons and the greater your chances of passing any test that life throws at you. This is important to note because there is no end to the tests and challenges you will face in life.

When my youngest son was in college, he became very frustrated with The Dating Game. He had been unable to find a fulfilling relationship and was becoming very discouraged in his efforts to find Ms. Right. I suggested to him that the problem might not be a shortage of prospects for companionship, but instead the problem might simply be a matter of preparedness. I asked him, *If I could somehow guarantee that you would find the companion of your dreams exactly two years from today, would you still be feeling the same level of discontent?* He responded by saying, "If I knew this to be true, I wouldn't be discontented; instead I'd just go about my daily life, calmly waiting to meet Ms. Right." I suggested that he do just that because his future companion might just be waiting on him. I then suggested that perhaps all he needed to do for the two of them to recognize one another was for him to exercise some patience by spending the next couple of years dating casually in order to learn more about love, intimacy and relationships. This would better prepare him for the kind of relationship that the woman he would be looking for really needs.

Through my ministry, I have frequently counseled individuals and couples who were struggling with life challenging issues. To me, it was often obvious that these individuals needed to make some fundamental changes in their lives. Interestingly enough, this was *rarely obvious* to those individuals. They didn't seem to grasp that if they wanted a different life experience, they would need to be prepared to see, do and think differently in order to make the changes necessary to have such an experience. In the words of Benjamin Franklin, "By failing to prepare, your are preparing to fail."

When who or what you need is not coming your way, ask yourself, "Am I sufficiently prepared for the life lessons and experiences coming from the Classroom, and if not, what changes or preparations do I need to make?"

The 3rd Key: Clear Your Mind - Sometimes your mind can become so cluttered that you can't think straight much less see clearly the next lesson or relationship from the Classroom. By "cluttered," I mean a mind so preoccupied with or crippled by stress, worry, uncertainty, fear or addiction issues that you are overwhelmed to the point that you aren't receptive to anyone or anything new or different. In addition, if you have a closed mind, you won't be open to new ideas - ideas that could free your mind to embrace your next opportunity.

There are any numbers of ways to open your mind and/or clear it of clutter or self-defeating thoughts. Some ways are harmful and short-lived (abusing alcohol and drugs), and others are beneficial and provide insight and clarity (prayer, introspection, meditation). Since you are already familiar with prayer, let's look briefly at simple meditation. Our minds, particularly when we are alone, unhappy or under stress, tend to jump rapidly from one thought to another, never focusing on any one thought long enough to provide any kind of resolution or change.

Meditation teachers refer to this as monkey mind. Meditation helps to calm this "monkey mind" long enough to attain clarity of thought. The reason for meditation is that one of the interesting things about the mind is that, even though it can generate thousands of thoughts per minute, it can only process one thought at a time. Consequently, a key objective of meditation is to cut down on the sheer volume of thoughts racing through your head. When you do this, it gives your mind a little breathing room so you can think more clearly and focus on any single problem or issue long enough to solve it. In essence, and to the degree that it is possible, the idea is one of thoughtless-ness, to have few if any thoughts racing through your head. In the words of mediation teacher Shunryn Suzikui, "If your mind is empty, it is always ready for anything; it is open to everything."

You can go on the Internet and find hundreds of short videos demonstrating various kinds of meditation. I suggest you look for Transcendental Meditation or TM. It's simple and is not tied to any religion, cult or ideology. You can also try my own meditation exercise. Find a comfortable sitting position in a quiet room and place a lighted candle at eye level about six feet in front of you. As you stare at the candle, focus your mind on your breath coming in and going out of your nose. When you slowly inhale, picture in your mind that breath being red. When you slowly exhale, picture that breath as being blue. While doing this, begin to slow down your breathing. What you want to do is take very deep breaths, slowly inhaling and exhaling until you are taking about 4-6 breaths per minute. Next, picture your mind as an empty theater stage. As thoughts pop up, view them as actors who have come onto your stage, acknowledge their presence and then tell them to leave. Then visualize these thoughts walking off the stage and refocus your mind on the candle and your breath. At first, you might be able to go thoughtless for only a few seconds, but with practice you can go longer. Be patient with this process, it takes a good bit of practice to still and quiet the mind.

One last thought related to clearing the mind. When you are feeling stressed about a life, career or spiritual path, there is a tendency to lie in bed at night worrying about what you are going to do. The clutter this creates in your mind is a leading cause of a poor night's sleep, and rarely solves your problem. I suggest that instead of worrying about that problem, completely empty your mind. This has two benefits: first, it allows for a better night's sleep, and second, it allows you to wake up refreshed and better prepared to address that problem. The way I quiet my mind at night is to limit myself to only 15-20 minutes for rehashing the day's events, thinking about tomorrow's concerns or regretting past decisions. If I did not set this 20 minute time limit, my mind would go on for hours, jumping from thought to thought. At the end of this time limit, I say to myself, "That's enough of that." I then start repeating the word sleep, sleep, sleep. When a worry or thought pops into my head, I immediately go back to repeating the word, sleep. This takes a bit of practice, but it is very effective.

When you find yourself facing a crisis, and your mind is filled with fear, worry or uncertainty, wait until you have cleared your mind before making a decision, and ask this question, "Is the reason I cannot focus on solutions because my mind is cluttered with stress, worry and uncertainty or because my mind is closed to any new ideas or lessons from the Classroom?"

The 4th Key: Allow for Construction - There will be times in your life when you believe you are ready to move on to the next lesson, but you can't understand why the opportunity has yet to present itself. Perhaps the problem is no longer one of openness or preparedness, but one of "construction." This is to say that, you are in fact receptive to and prepared for the next lesson from the Classroom, but the next experience may not be quite ready for you, and it is simply time to wait.

A personal example: My wife and I have talked frequently about how nice it would have been if we had met 20 years earlier. However, there was the possibility that we would not have been receptive to each other 20 years earlier. It is more likely that we needed to spend those years maturing and learning more about whom and what we needed from a marriage partner. In other words, it was a good thing that we had to wait because the relationship part of our lives had still been "under construction."

I have to admit that waiting is not one of my better virtues. In my 20s and 30s, when I found myself at a difficult crossroads, I would get depressed and stressed-out. When I began my Flash Point Experiment, and felt I was being receptive, but I couldn't see clearly how to proceed, I knew it was time to wait for the next life lesson or experience to present itself. When I find myself in this situation, I try to relax and live in the present by not wanting my situation or my circumstances to be something other than what they are. When you invite into your life the next lesson from the Classroom, but the path is not self-evident, sometimes it's simply a matter of timing because that experience is still under construction. When this proves to be the case, it is one of those times when you simply need to wait.

SUMMARY

III. EXTEND THE INVITATION: *Invite God to send you the life lessons, relationships, tools, ideas and opportunities that are most essential for personal growth, spiritual development and physical well-being - COME WHAT MAY.*

Step 3 is about bringing speedily into being the next life lesson or experience from God's Classroom without Walls that is essential for meeting your needs, solving your problems and fulfilling your purpose. In order to accelerate this process, it suggests that you drop your Checklist of Wants & Desires, invite God to reveal the next life lesson or experience, then Create the Conduits and receptivity necessary to bring that experience into being.

Before you began your Experiment, you might not have known

that all along that God has been providing you with the relationships and life lessons necessary for personal growth, spiritual development and physical well-being. Consequently, you might have limited your Personal Growth or life potential by ignoring, rejecting or avoiding some of those lessons. By Extending the Invitation, you now have a new perspective. A perspective that requires confidence and trust in God, and the receptivity necessary to view everyone and everything in your life as a lesson from God's Classroom without Walls that has come to teach you what's essential for meeting your needs. I am not suggesting that "everything happens for a reason" (because there are a lot of unreasonable things that can happen in life), but I am suggesting that there is something to learn from everyone and everything that happens in our lives.

The "How?" question we asked at the beginning of this chapter was, *How can I bring quickly into being the life lessons and experiences from the classroom that are most essential for meeting my needs, solving my problems and fulfilling my purpose?* The answer is simply to Extend the Invitation, and regardless of what it might cost you, always end this invitation by saying, COME WHAT MAY.

The most important lesson I learned from implementing Step 3 was that I bring into being the experience to which I am most receptive; whether this be to fulfill my worldly wants and desires or to meet my real needs. The sincerity of my invitation, and whether or not I really meant it when I say COME WHAT MAY, determines the nature and quality of that experience. The question of how long it is going to take, what price I will need to pay, and how much I will learn on my journey is directly proportional to my needs, the extent of my preparation and the degree of my receptivity.

I have also learned that many individuals are hesitant to extend this invitation because they fear change, don't want to drop their Checklist of Wants & Desires or their mind is not open to seeking God's Will. They would rather live in the discomfort of an unfulfilling life than risk entering uncharted territory populated with new or different experiences that might challenge their beliefs or threaten their current lifestyle.

You have now Extended the Invitation to bring into being the life lessons, relationships and experience you need, and have done your part to bring this into being. Step 4 will provide you the navigational tools and exercises necessary to attain the personal growth, spiritual development and physical well-being you need to meet your needs and solve your problems.

Step #4: Pay Attention

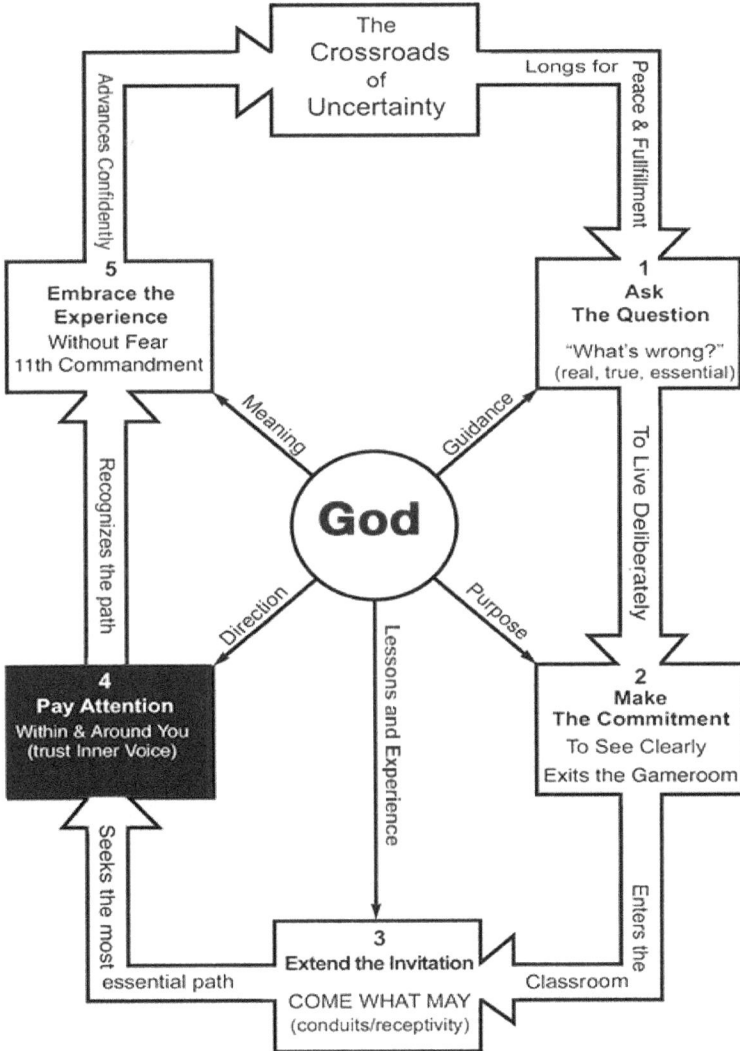

The
Crossroads
of
Uncertainty

Longs for

Advances Confidently

Peace & Fulfillment

5
Embrace the
Experience
Without Fear
11th Commandment

1
Ask
The Question
"What's wrong?"
(real, true, essential)

Recognizes the path

Meaning

Guidance

To Live Deliberately

God

Direction

Purpose

Lessons and Experience

4
Pay Attention
Within & Around You
(trust Inner Voice)

2
Make
The Commitment
To See Clearly
Exits the Gameroom

Seeks the most

essential path

3
Extend the Invitation
COME WHAT MAY
(conduits/receptivity)

Classroom

Enters the

© Copyright 2001 Baxter Castro Coffee

Chapter 4

Step Four: Pay Attention

PAY ATTENTION - *Pay attention to what is going on within and around you in order to recognize the path or course of action that will provide the experience necessary to meet your needs, solve your problems and fulfill you purpose.* To "recognize the path" creates a Flash Point that enables you to see clearly the direction your life needs to take. With this recognition comes the understanding of why this particular path is most essential for meeting your needs

"One cannot give oneself an aim or direction, I've already tried that countless times, and it did not work. One needs not to invent an aim, but to find one which is already in existence, and which I have but to recognize." Lev Nikolayevich Tolstoy, Russian novelist and philosopher

WHY PAY ATTENTION?

- Because you have established a sense of PURPOSE, and now long for a sense of DIRECTION. Paying conscious attention to what is going on within and around you, reveals the impressions, signs and signals that will provide that sense of direction.

- Not to pay attention is to ignore these "impressions, signs and signals." The root word for *ignore* is the same as the root word for *ignorance.* If you are not paying attention, you could remain in ignorance about which direction to turn or path to take.

- Because you have exercised your faith, the strength of your will and/or your logic and reason to find your way, but without the desired outcome. Consequently, you are looking for some new or at least different navigational tools.

- Another reason to pay attention is that you cannot fabricate God's Will because it already exists and needs only to be recognized. Without this recognition, you will not be able to discover the path or course of action that will provide the experience to meet your needs, solve your problems or fulfill your purpose.

When you commit to paying attention, you're acknowledging that there is something missing or not working in your life, and you need to cultivate the skills to recognize who or what this might be. After you have invited God to send the life lessons and experience you need, you now seek the path that will provide these lessons and that experience so you will be able to start meeting your needs and solving your problems. In addition, when you find yourself at a Crossroads of Uncertainty without a sense of direction, it's often because of the choices you've made. Consequently, you are looking for a different approach to making life decisions.

B. MY EXPERIENCE - After extending my second Invitation, I had no idea what next to expect. After coming off a year of disasters (my Great Train Wreck), there was a part of me that feared by again inviting God to send me who or what I needed (COME WHAT MAY no less), I would be hit by yet another string of calamities. Fortunately, this proved not to be the case. Instead, what happened was that a parade of very diverse people, ideas and opportunities began to march rapidly through my life. At first, I was excited about this barrage of new people, ideas and opportunities. However, over the ensuing months, I began to get overwhelmed and confused by the sheer number of paths, possibilities and choices coming my way because some of these were threatening to my secular and religious beliefs as well as my then current lifestyle.

As I began to apply the Reality Touchstone to evaluate these possibilities and choices, I came to realize that I was approaching the limits of my knowledge and experience. Once I invited God to send me the life lessons and experience I needed from the classroom, I next needed to find the path that would provide those lessons and that experience. Although I now had a sense of purpose, I didn't have the navigational tools I needed to attain sense of direction.

At that point, I began to question not only the life, career, religious and relationship choices that had led me to this particular crossroads, but also to question the choice-making process itself. As I thought about the choices I had made, it occurred to me that some of my best experience had come about without my having to make a choice. This is to say, there were times in my life when the lesson, relationship or experience I needed, was so obvious that no analysis, decision or conscious choice was necessary. I didn't need faith, logic, reason or the strength of my will to find it, I simply recognized the most essential path or course of action. Subsequently, my challenge became to find a way I could replicate this process at will.

The "How?" question I needed to answer was, *How do I determine which path or course of action will provide the life lessons and experience necessary to meet my needs, solve my problems and fulfill my purpose?*

B. The MAIN IDEAS – In Chapter 3, you invited God to send you the life lessons and experience necessary to attain personal growth, spiritual development and physical well-being, and you cultivated the necessary conduits and receptivity to bring this into being. The reason for attaining these is that, they are the primary resources you will draw upon to meet your needs, solve your problems and fulfil your purpose. As you strive to find the path that will provide these lessons and experience, this chapter will provide you with the navigational tools you need to recognize the direction that leads to this path.

Step 4 is about establishing a sense of direction and re-thinking the decision-making process. The direction necessary to find your most essential relationship, career or spiritual path, and an alternate way of making decisions about the choices and opportunities that will come with these paths. As stated in Chapter 2, I have on occasion suggested a broad, temporary PURPOSE for our seminar participants, at least until they have established one of their own. However, I would be very hesitant to suggest a specific DIRECTION for my readers to follow because I don't know where they are coming from or going to. What I can do is share some proven navigational tools that myself and others have used to attain this sense of direction. "Efforts and courage are not enough without purpose and direction." President John F. Kennedy

A sense of DIRECTION is the second component of the **Third Theme of Primessentialism,** with the other two being PURPOSE and MEANING. There is not one singular path in life, but there is an overall direction, e.g. there are spiritual paths, career paths, relationship paths, etc. At any given point in your life, you might be making forward progress on one path, while you are simultaneously making little headway on another path. Nevertheless, as long as you are moving in the right direction, you will ultimately recognize the path(s) that will provide the experience necessary to meet your needs.

In Chapter 3, you cultivated the necessary conduits as well as the receptivity to bring into being the lessons and experience from the Classroom for meeting your needs. As you strive to find the path that will provide those lessons, and that experience, this chapter will provide you with the navigational tools you need to recognize the direction that leads to this path.

Establishing a sense of DIRECTION is the 2nd Prerequisite for making your life complete. Without a sense of direction, you won't know how to get from where you are to where you need to be. You will not find the path or course of action that will provide the life lessons and relationship experience necessary to attain balance in your life. A balanced life will empower you with the clarity, means and ideas to start meeting your needs, solving your problems and fulfilling your purpose.

Establishing a Sense of Direction

As you strive to attain a sense of direction, there are two key points to keep in mind. The first point is that, the path or course of action you are looking for is not necessarily your final destination. However, you can discover the next step in that direction. To illustrate this point, I don't think it would have been emotionally possible for me to jump immediately from my divorce to my second marriage. I first needed to transition through a number of relationships before I gained the insight and understanding to prepare me for my relationship with my now remarkable wife.

This same concept also applied to my career path. I first had to transition through a number of less-than-ideal jobs before I gained the knowledge and experience necessary for my current career as a business consultant. The same with my spiritual path. I had to transition through a number of religious ideologies before I began my prison ministry. What you are looking for is the path or course of action that will provide the experience necessary to become all that God knows you are capable of being.

The second key point is that what you are looking for is not necessarily the easiest, most desirable or acceptable path. What you are looking for is who or what is next to facilitate your efforts to find your most essential path. This path might bring lessons that are challenging or difficult or it might bring lessons that are rich and fulfilling; one in which you learn a lot about yourself as well as about love, life and spirituality. As mentioned, the nature and quality of your experience depends on your needs, the level of your preparedness and the degree of your receptivity.

Still others might have chosen a path or relationship based solely on their wants and desires or the expectations of others, instead of choosing to seek guidance from God. A path that did little to provide the sense of direction needed to find their next or most essential path. To facilitate your efforts to attain a sense of direction, this chapter will:

- Demonstrate the futility of trying to fabricate a reality or invent a true sense of direction or course of action (WHAT I'VE LEARNED).
- Stress the need to exercise courage as you make progress with your Flash Point Experiment (THE QUESTION).
- Emphasize how paying conscious attention to what is going on within and around you will facilitate your efforts to find the path that will provide the experience necessary to attain personal growth, spiritual development and physical well-being. (ACTION ITEM #1).

- Introduce the Early Warning and Internal Guidance Systems as well as the Recognition Factor, and the role these navigational tools play in providing a sense of direction. (ACTION ITEMS #2 & #3)
- Introduce the Perils & Pitfalls of Choice. (ACTIOM ITEM #4)

D. WHAT I'VE LEARNED - *That which is real, true and essential cannot be fabricated or invented – it can only be recognized. The recognition of "what is" brings the understanding of "what needs to be."* - "A man should look for what is and not for what he thinks should be." Albert Einstein

This **4th Primessential Principle** suggests that reality and truth already exist – they only need to be recognized, and with this recognition will come the understanding of why this needs to be. For instance: Isaac Newton didn't invent the gravitational pull of the earth, he simply recognized how it worked, and gave it a name: The Law of Gravity. With this *recognition* came the *understanding* necessary for Newton to see its application to the natural world. This is to suggest that, the answers to many of your questions, and the solutions to many of your problems already exist, they simply need to be recognized or discovered.

We sometimes deceive ourselves by attempting to invent or fabricate a belief system, reality or personality to help us navigate through life and relationships. For example, if you are a woman and you feel heartbroken over a recent breakup, that is your reality. Consequently, you might invent a tough "I'm-not-going-to-be-hurt-again" persona. Although this tough-girl persona might keep you from being hurt in the future, it could also keep you from finding true love in the present. I say this because people will not be seeing or dating the real you, but only the tough you (which isn't who you really are, but simply an invented personality to help you survive). It is only an authentic or True Self that can experience a true love.

We can arbitrarily choose a path or direction for our lives, but the true path to a meaningful life, healthy relationships and a fulfilling spiritual path can only be recognized (although occasionally it can be stumbled upon). In the words of the Cubist painter, Georges Braque, "Truth exists, only falsehood has to be invented."

Here is one example of my applying this principle in my own life. After my divorce, I invited God to help me recognize the marriage partner who would be most essential for supporting my Flash Point Experiment. Following this invitation, I did my best to create the necessary conduits and receptivity to bring this to fruition, e.g. I told friends and family I was looking for a companion, attended social functions at my church and joined online dating sites. During this time, I tried my best to keep an open mind in order to increase my receptivity to whatever relationship might come my way. As time ticked by, I became increasingly desperate in my search because I wanted each new person I dated to be The One. When I finally did meet my future wife, I immediately *recognized* that she was "The One." In the months and years following this recognition, I came to *understand* clearly, why she was The One by the many ways in which she has met my needs and filled the void in my life. I should point out that, although you might immediately recognize the path that leads to companionship, it might take weeks or months after that relationship has begun (or ended) before you will understand why any given relationship experience has come with that path.

When you seek God's Will, you will be able to *recognize* the direction that leads to your next career, relationship or spiritual path, the ability to *recognize what is* - the awareness of what is going on within and around you, requires you to pay conscious attention. The word, conscious means to be aware of and responding to one's surroundings; to be fully awake. This kind of attention will enable you to *understand what needs to be* - why this particular path, lesson, person or course of action is the next, best or most essential direction. In the pages to follow, we will explore the need to exercise courage when applying this principle and provide the navigational tools you need to find your next or most essential path.

E. THE QUESTION - *When the path or course of action presents itself, will I have the courage to follow it, regardless of where it might lead or what price I might have to pay? -* "Courage is the power to let go of the familiar." Raymond Lindquist, Presbyterian minister

Once you have Extended the Invitation, there is a high probability that the path or course of action that is most essential for supporting your Flash Point Experiment might lead you into unfamiliar territory. It will require a great deal of courage to follow this path because it could possibly require you to break from the herd, go against the tide of popular opinion or exit the Matrix. For some people, this path might be only a slight detour from their current path. For others, it could lead them in a dramatically different direction. This new direction could bring new experiences that would alter significantly how they see themselves, their secular or religious beliefs, or their existing circumstances and station in life.

Why courage? It takes courage to admit that there is something missing or not working in your life and acknowledge that there might need to be some significant changes in your Worldview, beliefs and/or lifestyle. It takes faith, confidence and courage to drop your Checklist of Wants & Desires and trust that God will lead you to who and what you need at this stage of your life. It takes courage to expand your Database of Knowledge & Experience to include new people and explore new ideas and activities. It takes courage to not settle for just any experience. It takes courage to Extend the Invitation and truly mean it when you say COME WHAT MAY. Most importantly, it takes courage to be your True Self, in a world that is trying to make you everybody else.

Whether one is climbing a mountain, social climbing or climbing the corporate ladder, there are any numbers of ways to get from where you are to where you need to be. Some paths will just require more courage. We could define courage as, *The ability to face difficulty, uncertainty, change or the unknown, not without fear, but in spite of that fear.* For instance, a courageous soldier going into battle would naturally fear for her life, but nonetheless she advances in spite of her fear because her only two options are courage or cowardice. In the words of Mark Twain, "Courage is resistance to fear, mastery of fear – not absence of fear."

My experience with courage has often come by default. I say this because there have been times in my life when I have found myself at a Crossroads of Uncertainty, and the only options I had left were to exercise courage, quit or fail. To illustrate, when I was 30 years old, I realized that my salary as a college professor was not going to meet the needs of my growing family, and I was terrified of trying to find a completely different career path. You might have faced a similar fear when you were laid off from your job, became disillusioned with your spiritual path or struggled through a divorce. Regardless of my fears and lack of business experience, the only options I had left were either to allow my fears to overwhelm me or exercise the courage that leads to action. In Chapter 5 we will provide some proven tools for managing one's fears.

I should add that I don't consider myself to be a particularly courageous person, but when I am faced with adversity, uncertainty or fear of the unknown, I've learned that,

There is *always* a way to get from where I am are to where I need to be.

F. THE ACTION ITEMS - "We need to pay attention; our world, both inner and outer, always tells us what is going on." Gloria

Karpinski, *Where Two Worlds Touch*

The ACTION ITEMS in Step 4 will help you bring into being a sense of direction by encouraging you to pay conscious attention to what is going on in your world, "both inner and outer." ACTION ITEMS #1 and #2 will assist your efforts to attain a better sense of direction. As you follow this direction, ACTION ITEM #3 will help you recognize the path or course of action that will provide the life lessons, relationships and experience to continue meeting your needs and solving your problems. You might not immediately find your ideal companion, career or spiritual path but at least you will be taking a step in the right direction. In addition, there will be times when you will not be able to make a decision or attain a sense of direction because you have been getting in your own way. This is often due to the choices you make. Consequently, this chapter will conclude by introducing the Perils & Pitfalls of Choice.

I mentioned earlier that logic, reason, and analyzing facts and information were the primary tools we use to identify and solve problems. However, many individuals who have attended our seminars tell us they have used these tools to the best of their ability, but still lack a sense of direction. In this section, we will provide your with some alternate navigational tools. These tools will utilize one of the 4 Elements of your Database of Knowledge & Experience - sensory perception, e.g. seeing, listening and feeling. These navigational tools will help you attain a better sense of direction. These tools are not designed to replace faith, logic or reason, but to supplement these by paying keen attention to what is going on within and around you. I've learned that, me direction in life is never static, I am always either moving toward or way from my most essential path.

These ACTION ITEMS will provide three different, but related navigational tools that will help you to attain a better sense of direction. These tools will enable you to understand what is taking place within you and what is going on around you in order to pick up on the signs, signals and impressions from God that are pointing you in the right direction:

1. **The Early Warning System**
2. **Your Internal Guidance System**
3. **The Recognition Factor**

In addition there will be times when you will not be able to make a decision or attain a sense of direction because you have been getting in your own way.

ACTION ITEM #1: Pay Conscious Attention - "The ability to observe without judgment is the highest form of intelligence."- Juddu Krishnamurti, 20th Century spiritual leader

This first "navigational tool" will encourage you to pay conscious attention to what is taking place *around you.* Conscious attention is about "observing without judgment" (without comparing it to past experience or someone else's experience), and looking or listening with a concerted effort long enough to grasp the essence of whom or what you are experiencing.

To grasp the essence of someone or something is to grasp its intrinsic nature by observing and understanding what it really is, what it's about and what that means (its significance).

Paying conscious attention to what is taking place around you will enable you to wake up and see life, yourself and others as they really are; the reality of your current circumstances or station in life. The reason for this is that, you can't establish a sense of direction until you first know where you are in life. To illustrate, let's say that you called me and said that your problem was how to get to Houston, Texas. The first thing I would ask you is, *Where are you now?* If you didn't know where you were it would not be possible for me to provide the direction necessary to get you from where you are to where you need to be. In a similar vein, if you don't pay conscious attention to where you are in life - your current ideas and beliefs as well as your current circumstances and station in life, you won't be able to recognize which direction to turn or path to take in order to change those ideas, beliefs and circumstances or improve your station in life.

To Pay Conscious Attention is to be completely awake, fully conscious and aware of what is taking place around you. Someone once asked the Buddha if he was God, and he said, "No," if he was a prophet, and he said, "No." When asked if he was a great teacher, he said, *"No."* Out of frustration, he asked the Buddha, Well if you're not God, a prophet or teacher, what are you? The Buddha replied, "I am awake."

Needless to say, I am no Buddha. Quite the contrary, it wasn't until I was 20 years old that I discovered I had not been "awake" for most of my life. Like most narcissistic young adults, I had paid very little conscious attention to what was taking place in the world around me.

What made me aware of this was a bus tour I took with my fellow art students in 1970 to visit the major art museums in the Midwest. One morning outside of Chicago, as the bus pulled over to refuel, I stepped outside the bus and saw a very remarkable sunrise. As I looked at that sunrise, the thought occurred to me that I had never actually "seen" or been consciously aware of a sunrise. Up until that point in my life I had *looked* at many sunrises, but for the first time in my life, it was as if the eyes of my understanding were opened and I could see clearly the beauty and *essence of sunrise-ness*. (Ephesians 1:18)

Conscious Attention is an important skill to cultivate because God is always providing you with signs, signals, impressions and clues, and if you are not paying attention you could miss out on this guidance and direction. The purpose of ACTION ITEM #1 is to encourage you to wake up and pay conscious attention to what is taking place *around you* by really Seeing, Listening and Feeling rather than merely Describing, Judging and Filing your life experience.

PAYING CONSCIOUS ATTENTION

Describing/Judging/Filing vs. Seeing/Listening/Feeling

Motivational speaker Werner Erhard has suggested that from early childhood we begin to learn how to assess problems by processing facts and information - that is, *Describing, Judging* and *Filing* those facts and that information. Describing, judging and filing information enables our brains to organize and prioritize information about people, circumstances and events. We *describe* the apparent facts about people, events or things in our life, e.g. old or young, tall or short, attractive or unattractive, etc. We next make a *judgment,* e.g. good or bad, right or wrong, acceptable or unacceptable, etc. We then *file* this information for future use, e.g. important or unimportant, useful or useless, safe or dangerous, etc. There is nothing inherently wrong with gathering information, analyzing facts and making judgments about your life, career, relationship or spiritual path. However, just analyzing your experience does not necessarily mean you are actually processing, interpreting, internalizing or learning by this experience.

I once worked for a group of behavioral scientists from whom I learned that research has determined 47% of the time individuals don't pay attention to what is going on around them. We are simply Describing, Judging and Filing what is taking place, but not paying attention enough to determine who or what it is, what they or it is about, or what this means. We are simply running on Automatic Pilot and not really interpreting, internalizing or paying attention to whom we are with, what we are thinking, believing or doing, or where we're at in life. Paying Conscious attention is a valuable skill to learn because we tend to see what we want to see and disregard the rest.

Instead of just *Describing, Judging* and *Filing* your life experience, make the effort to pay conscious attention to whom or what is in front of you. One way to do this is to use your senses to really *See, Listen a*nd *Feel* what's going on around you without wanting your situation to be something other than what it is or the person you are with to be someone they are not. Describing, judging and filing your life experience is a logical and rational approach for gaining insight and understanding. Seeing, listening your life experience is an emotional and sensory perception approach to gaining insight and understanding.

Limiting yourself to just one of these approaches will hinder your ability to attain a clear sense of direction.

Unless you have taken some psychology or drawing classes, you have probably had very little, if any training on how to see, much less listen or feel, what is taking place around you. To remedy this, ACTION ITEM #1 will introduce an elementary overview of these three tools, as well as exercises to improve your ability to use your sensory perception to pay conscious attention to what is going on *around* you.

a. To *see* more consciously (looking vs. seeing): In Chapter 2 we introduced the value of Making the Commitment to See Clearly. This section will expand on the value of seeing things as they really are instead of how you think they are or want them to be. Looking is basically a visual perception process in which you analyze the apparent facts or physical attributes of a person, place or thing, e.g. it's color, shape, size, etc. On the other hand, *seeing* is cognition or insight. It's about how clearly or how well you interpret whom or what you are looking at. Looking is a passive process, whereas seeing requires conscious attention. To "see" is a both a visual perception process (*I see a tree.*) and a comprehension process (*I can see what this is about. I can see where this is going. I can see your point.*). To comprehend someone or something is to look at them or it long enough and objectively enough until you can grasp the essence of who or what they are about. *"It's not what you look at that matters, it's what you see."* Henry David Thoreau, *Walden*

Earlier I gave an example of my grasping the essence of a sunrise. Here is another example of grasping the essence of something. My brother used to race dirt bikes (motorcycles). Although he has no formal art training, he can draw a very accurate rendition of a motorcycle from his visual memory. He can draw a side view, a front view and a rear view of a motorcycle with meticulous detail. The reason he can do this is that he has grasped the *essence of motorcycle-ness.* He has taken them apart, put them back together, and ridden them so many times that he can clearly see them in his "mind's eye." In other words, he has not just *looked* at motorcycles; he has actually *seen* motorcycles. On the other hand, my brother, like most of the population, cannot draw a tree very well even though he has looked at hundreds of thousands of trees in his lifetime. The difference in the two being that he has grasped the *essence of motorcycle-ness,* but not the *essence of tree-ness.* Like most people, he has looked at thousands of trees in his lifetime, but has failed to pay conscious attention to them – to actually *see* a tree.

Here is a simple exercise to improve your ability to see the essence of someone or something. Look at an object or person you see on a regular basis and pretend you have never seen it before. We could use the "essence of tree-ness" for this exercise. Look at a tree and focus on its shape, the texture of its bark, the shape and color of its leaves, its size compared to other trees, the relationship in size between the trunk and its branches and whether its roots go directly into the ground (like a palm tree) or spread out away from the tree (like an oak tree). Next, walk up to that tree and give it a good smell and then hug it in order to feel its mass, energy and strength. This exercise will help you to pay more conscious attention to what constitutes a tree, and will improve your efforts to grasp the essence of tree-ness. The purpose of this exercise is to create a Flash Point - the point where you realize there might be 100s or even 1,000s of people and things in your life that you have only looked at, but not really *seen*, and to which you need to pay more conscious attention.

Another aspect of paying conscious attention is to see, not just what is there, but to also see what is not there. This is a very valuable skill for meeting your needs and solving your problems because there will be times when you are looking for a solution to a particular problem but it's not something that is obvious, but something that is missing; something you are not seeing or something that is *not* there. The inability to notice what is going on around you might cause you to overlook the visuals signs and clues that God is providing to give you a sense of direction.

b. To *listen* more consciously (hearing vs. listening): To *hear* is simply a physical response to auditory vibrations (*I can hear you talking.*). To *listen* is to pay conscious attention to people speaking in order to internalize or interpret what they are about or what they mean *(I hear you loud and clear, I understand what you mean." I hear what you are saying.*). Hearing is also a passive process, whereas listening requires conscious attention. To illustrate this point, visualize yourself at a party and walking through a large room of 60 people with dozens of conversations taking place. You can *hear* everyone talking, but you are unable to grasp what they are actually saying. However, if you stop for a minute and pay conscious attention to any one individual, you can then *listen* to her conversation and understand what she is saying.

Another reason for conscious listening is that sociologists have determined that poor listeners are not actually listening while the other person is speaking. Instead, they are merely hearing the other person talking, and just biding their time, formulating in their minds what they are going to say when it is their turn to speak. "Most people do not listen with the intent to understand; they listen with the intent to reply."

Stephen R Covey, *7 Habits of Highly Successful People*

The French mathematician and Christian apologist, Blaise Pascal once observed, "I have often said that man's unhappiness arises from one thing only, namely that he cannot abide quietly in one room."

It's been my observation that many individuals cannot bear the "sound of silence" They can't stand to be alone with their thoughts or feelings, either sitting in their living room, working at their desk or driving in their car.

They always have to have some kind of background noise like the radio, television or mobile devices to distract them from their thoughts. I have often been guilty of this while watching television, and when a commercial comes on, I reach for my phone and scan social media sites. Unfortunately, this background noise prevents me from hearing the subtle signals coming from my Inner Voice which could provide me with a measure of direction. The French mathematician and Christian apologist, Blaise Pascal once observed, "I have often said that man's unhappiness arises from one thing only, namely that he cannot abide quietly alone in one room."

When I was in college, I once had a roommate who would come home from class and immediately turn on the television. He did this, not because there was a television show he wanted to watch, but just to add some "background noise" to his life. To improve your listening skills, drop the background noise and give up the need to be entertained or distracted every minute of every day. Be patient; conscious listening takes practice. To more easily listen to what's taking place around you, try sitting quietly in a room for just 10 minutes without the television or stereo on, or using your cell phone, in order to hear your own thoughts as well as the promptings from your Inner Voice.

In addition, on your morning commute to school or work, make that drive without listening to the radio. To improve your listening skills, try sitting outside with a pen and paper for 10 minutes and make the conscious effort to record how many different sounds you can list that are coming from your neighborhood. When you first try this, you might not hear that much, but with conscious listening you can hear birds singing, leaves rustling, air conditioners humming, construction workers building a house, airplanes overhead, dogs barking, children playing, cars passing, etc. When others are speaking, conscious listening helps you to more easily hear the message behind their words.

Like conscious seeing, conscious listening enables you to hear not only what people are saying, but also to be mindful of what they are *not* saying. You can often learn a lot about a person by paying conscious attention to what they are *not* saying. Paying Conscious Attention to what people are or are not saying, can provide valuable clues to their real agenda; clues we might miss if we are not really listening.

Listening consciously to what is going on around you, enables you to notice the subtle auditory signals that can facilitate your efforts to attain a clear sense of direction. For instance, you might be a single woman eating at a restaurant and hear dozens of conversations taking place around you. However, when you pay conscious attention to the conversations coming from the table next to yours you can listen to what they are saying. From this, you learn that one of the women at that table found the job of her dreams by using a particular online job posting site. Perhaps this had never occurred to you, but from listening to that conversation, you now have a new direction to investigate. The inability to listen to what is going on around you might cause you to overlook the auditory signals from others, your surroundings or your Inner Voice that could provide you with a new sense of direction.

c. To *feel* more consciously (analyzing vs, feeling): Although our feelings are something that take place within us, the feelings I am talking about in this ACTION ITEM are those we experience in response to someone or something that is taking place around us. Analyzing facts is one way we internalize what is going on around us. Our feelings are another way we internalize what is going on around us, so paying conscious attention to what these feelings are telling us can provide a measure of guidance and direction. In order to glean the most benefit from your feelings, bear in mind the following concept:

No one can *make* you feel anything; you alone determine how you are going to allow yourself to feel about any given person, conversation or circumstance that is taking place around you.

Eleanor Roosevelt once said, "No one can make you feel inferior without your consent." In fact, no one can make you feel anything (happy, glad, sad, angry, etc.) without your consent. If you allow someone else to dictate how you should feel, then this could negatively affect the direction you take in life. For example, you might feel strongly about a specific career, relationship or spiritual path, but if your friends or family question those feelings you might begin to doubt your own feelings. This doubt could influence you *not* to pursue a path that could have facilitated your efforts to meet your needs, solve your problems or provide a sense of direction.

Many of our seminar participants have shared with us that one of the most challenging concepts of Primessentialism is that they alone determine how they will feel about what is going on around them. To illustrate this point, during a seminar I sometimes walk up to someone sitting on the front row and gently kick that person on the knee. Some in my audience might feel this is very funny, and other might feel it is very inappropriate. The point being is that everyone saw the same action, but some *allowed* themselves to feel humor, while others *allowed* themselves to feel irritation. In other words, what we allow ourselves to feel is simply a choice - no one outside of ourselves can mandate our feelings.

There are two points to consider when paying conscious attention to your feelings. The first point I have mentioned - no one can make you feel anything you don't give yourself permission to feel. The second is that paying conscious attention to your feelings can serve as a kind of Early Warning System that can provide guidance and direction.

The Early Warning System

A wise person once said that our feelings reflect our true understanding about what we're experiencing, regardless of what we might intellectualize about them. This is crucial because our feelings can often provide us with guidance and direction before our logical mind can assess the facts of a given person or situation. These feelings serve as a kind of "Early Warning System" that precedes logic and analysis and can provide a sense of direction. For instance, you might be talking at length at a business meeting and suddenly get the feeling that you are boring your audience although no one has implied this. You might be sitting in your living room while your baby is in another room, and you get a strong feeling that you need to attend to her, even though she is not crying. You might be racing to the airport and get the feeling you need to slow down, although you see no immediate danger.

Your Early Warning System is similar, but different from your intuition. It is similar in the sense that they are both feelings, but your intuition is simply a hunch or gut feeling based on previous experience. Whereas, the feelings I am talking about are those in response to something taking place in the here and now. Paying conscious attention to your Early Warning System enables you to understand more easily what is going on around you. For example:

- It enables you to learn from *feelings of caution*- when someone or something seems too good to be true.
- It enables you to learn from *feelings of certainty* - even when friends and family are critical of the career, relationship or spiritual path you have chosen to follow.
- It enables you to learn from *feelings of doubt* – when your logic and reason tells you a prospective path or course of action is perfect for you, but your Early Warning System is telling you there is something not quite right about this direction, and you need to proceed carefully.

ACTION ITEM #2: Heed your Internal Guidance System

"There are many who find what they are seeking; they find clues that set them in the right direction." James L. Christian, *Philosophy, The Art of*

Wondering

ACTION ITEM #1 was about cultivating the skills necessary to pay conscious attention to what is going on *around you*. ACTION ITEM #2 will facilitate your efforts to bring into being a better sense of direction by encouraging you to tune-in to what is going on *within you*. This second "navigational tool" is what I refer to as one's Internal Guidance System. Your Early Warning System is about paying attention to your feelings; your Internal Guidance System is about attaining a sense of direction via signs, signals and impressions.

Your Internal Guidance System

This Internal Guidance System operates somewhat like a compass. It could be likened to the childhood game of "warmer/colder" in the sense that it can point you toward or away from a path or course of action by guiding you with:

- **Green Lights**
- **Red Flags**
- **Big Thumpers**

When you are seeking your next or most essential path, you might receive "Green Lights" to let you know that you're getting warmer - closer to finding your next life lesson or experience. This will be accompanied by feelings of peace, clarity and absolute certainty, even if this runs counter to your ideas and beliefs, and even if your logical mind questions the viability of that direction or course of action. If you ignore, or start moving away from this opportunity, you will might receive Red Flags to let you know that you are getting colder - going in the wrong direction. These Red Flags will be accompanied by feelings of doubt, confusion and/or uncertainty. To continue to ignore these Red Flags can lead to Big Thumpers, e.g. a toxic relationship, hurtful breakup, accident, heart attack, incarceration, divorce, addiction issues, etc. These ":Big Thumpers" are life's way (God's way) of getting your attention.

Here's simple illustration: If you are a man, and smile at a woman, and she smiles back, that is a Green Light - a visual sign to move forward. If you speak to her and she speaks back, that is another Green Light – an auditory signal to keep moving forward. If you try to kiss her and she slaps your face that is definitely a Red Flag - a physical sign to stop moving in that direction. If you ignore this particular Red Flag, you could get a Big Thumper - perhaps a conk on the head from her boyfriend. Your Internal Guidance System is not about your feelings, but is an internal system that can recognize the signs, signals and clues about the direction you are going.

Although there will be times when these Green Lights and Red Flags will be very obvious or even glaring, for the most part they are very subtle impressions, and will require you to pay conscious attention to who or what you are experiencing. This kind of conscious attention brings instant insight and clarity. I liken this "insight and clarity" to what the psychologist William James referred to as, "Noetic Truth: an impression of absolute certainty that something is true in the absence of concrete proof." In other words, your Internal Guidance System can provide you with feelings of certainty about a given career, relationship or spiritual path, even though your logic and reason are challenging that direction or the facts at hand run counter to what you are feeling. Although it takes a little practice to tune-in to these subtle signs. clues and signals, each time you heed them, and this bears fruit, the greater confidence you will have in this System.

One reason that some individuals can't pay attention to the promptings of their Internal Guidance System is because their minds have been dulled with addictive drugs, alcohol or from abusing prescription medicine. When I conduct seminars in treatment centers for recovering addicts, I tell them that the reason they shouldn't abuse alcohol or drugs isn't so much that this is wrong, addictive, unhealthy or even illegal. A better reason is that the abuse of alcohol and drugs can blur one's ability to pick up on the subtle promptings from their Internal Guidance System. In other words, alcohol or drugs are not inherently wrong or bad, but to abuse them could dull their ability to grasp the impressions, signs and signals coming from God. When these substances are abused, it's difficult to find, and easy to lose, your sense of direction.

It's been my observation that those who don't believe in an Internal Guidance System can't believe that those who do actually receive any guidance or direction. However, just because they haven't tapped into this System doesn't mean it doesn't exist, it only means they have yet to pay attention to it.

ACTION ITEM #3: Cultivate the Recognition Factor -
"Listen to your inward voice and bravely obey that." Ralph Waldo Emerson, *Self-Reliance and Other Essays*

Of all the ways of attaining a sense of direction or course of action, ACTION ITEM #3 is the most accurate, consistent and productive. As you start paying conscious attention to what is going on within and around you, you will improve your ability to recognize the feelings, impressions and signals that will facilitate your efforts to attain a clear sense of direction. As you follow this direction, ACTION ITEM #3 will help you identify your next or most essential path by introducing the Recognition Factor, and the role this third "navigational tool" plays in attaining a clear sense of direction.

The Recognition Factor

In his book, *Be Here Now, Now Be Here,* Baba Ram Dass made the following observation, "You may have reasoned and reasoned until you saw the peculiar position that rational man is in and you realized that there must be something else, although you have not experienced it." I would suggest that this "something else" could be the Recognition Factor. The Recognition Factor is about paying attention to your Inner Voice; a dynamic that incorporates your Inner Voice with the 4th Primessential Principle: *The recognition of what is, brings the understanding of what need to be.*

Your Inner Voice springs from your True Self, and your True Self is always attuned to God's Will. To benefit from this guidance and direction, it will be necessary to trust this voice in order to recognize what is, so you can understand what needs to be.

The scriptures teach that, "The kingdom of God is within you." Luke 17:21 In other words, the way to receive guidance and direction from God is not to look for something that is outside of you, but something that is within you. So, if you want to know God's Will for your life, you will need to turn inward, and pay attention to that "…still small voice" within – your Inner Voice. This inward journey is about paying attention to your Inner Voice so it can lead you to the path that will provide the ideas, lessons and experience you need to meet your needs and solve your problems. "Your mind knows only something. Your inner voice knows everything. If you listen, it will always lead you down the right path." Henry Winkler, actor and producer

The word, *recognize*, consists of the Latin terms, "re" which means *again*, and "cognize" which means *to know*; therefore, to *re-cognize* means *to know again.* What I am suggesting is that, on a very deep level there is something inside you that always knows the direction or course of action that's needed to meet your needs, answer your questions and provide a sense of direction. All you need to do to tap into this "something" is to pay attention to this Voice. "Your inner voice speaks loudly…until you ignore it so much it is nothing more than a whisper in your ear, waiting…" Dee Emkay, from the website, *The Mind's Journal*

When I use the term, Inner Voice I don't mean your conscience because your conscious isn't neutral, and it's a feeling not a voice. Your conscience is biased because it has been shaped by the beliefs, values and doctrines of your family, religion or the Matrix which might or might not be accurate or credible. If these beliefs and values are credible then your conscience would be an asset, if not, it could be convoluted, distorted, if not completely irrational, and lead you in the wrong direction. For example, if your family taught you that drinking alcoholic beverages was "wrong," your conscience would cause you to feel very guilty if you did drink alcohol. If your family does drink alcoholic beverages, your conscience would not bother you if you drank alcohol. The alcohol was neutral, it was one's conscience that made its consumption right or wrong.

Unlike your Internal Guidance System, the Recognition Factor doesn't rely on a sign, signal or impression. Instead, it's literally the voice inside your head that provides guidance and direction, even in the face of your logic and reason or your beliefs. The way to tell if this voice is from God or from a dark, malevolent force like insanity or schizophrenia is that, your Inner Voice will only tell you things that are legal, moral or essential to your personal growth, spiritual development and physical well-being. This voice is a clear statement that provides specific, concrete guidance and direction, e.g. Go here/Don't go there, turn here/stop now, pay attention to this/ignore that, or this is who or what's next, etc. Your Inner Voice provides this guidance and direction by telling you some variation of, *No, not here, not now, not this - this direction will hamper your forward progress.* For example, you might be dating a man you really like, but don't want to see any of his faults because he matches all the idealized attributes on your Checklist of Wants & Desires. However, your Inner Voice keeps telling you that, *He's not The One.*

When you Inner Voice points you toward or away from a relationship, path or course of action, you experience a Flash Point - the point where you instantly recognize whom or what's next. With this recognition, will come the understanding of why this particular lesson, relationship or experience is essential for meeting your needs and solving your problems. The way to tell if this voice is from God or from a malevolent force like insanity of schizophrenia is that your Inner Voice will only tell you something that is legal, moral or essential to your personal growth, spiritual development or physical well-being.

In her memoir, *A Piece of Cake,* Cupcake Brown wrote about her experiences with her Inner Voice: "I'd heard this Voice periodically. During my running-away escapades, it would direct me with things like: *Don't get in that car,* or *Don't go that way, or this way*, or *Don't go to that party.* I never really questioned who was the speaker or why it spoke. One thing was apparent though, whenever I didn't listen to it, I regretted it."

In addition, when I write about The Recognition Factor, I am not talking about the choice-making process. Making choices requires that you first gather as much information as you can about a given problem, situation or circumstance. You then analyze and prioritize that information, think or pray about your options, apply logic and reason, and then decide which option you think best. Whereas the Recognition Factor does not rely on analysis, logic and reason, requires little faith and doesn't necessitate a choice to be made. It's simply a matter of paying attention to "...the still small voice" in your head. When you pay keen attention to your Inner Voice, you won't need to struggle with a decision because you will recognize the path or course of action that is often self-evident. One advantage of the Recognition Factor over choice is in the immediacy of its application:

- You don't have to wait until you have all the facts at hand.

- You don't have to wait until you have overcome your guilt, shame or shortcomings in order to feel worthy of guidance and direction from God.
- You don't have to wait until you have worked through all your psychological pain, drama or addiction to receive clarity and insight.
- You don't have to wait until you feel all your sins have been forgiven before you can seek God's Will.
- You don't have to wait until you have logically analyzed every conceivable option before you can make a decision or attain a sense of direction.

Another advantage of the Recognition Factor over choice comes into play when it is time to make a decision, but there is no way to know the wisdom or folly of that decision until some point in the distant future. For example, the process of buying a home, choosing a career or spiritual path or deciding on a marriage partner. I would suggest that the career path that's most fulfilling for you to experience already exists - all you have to do is recognize it. The neighborhood that can best meet the needs of your family already exists - all you have to do is recognize it. The path to bliss, nirvana and salvation already exists - all you have to do is recognize it. The person you are going to marry has already been born, so all you have to do is recognize her. Sometimes this recognition will be immediate; at other times it will come as you learn more about that person.

Having stated the above, I would like to make one point very clear. There is *not* just one career, relationship, neighborhood or spiritual path for meeting your needs, there are many possibilities. For example, when looking for a marriage partner, there is not just one, Mr. Right. What you are looking for is Mr. Right Now. This could be *no* relationship at this time, a *transitional* relationship or *the* relationship. I've learned that, my Inner Voice already knows the way - all I have to do is trust it.

ACTION ITEM #4: Practice Choice-less Awareness - "The man of control lives in choice, and the man of understanding lives in choiceless-ness." Buddhist saying

ACTION ITEM #4 is about the decision-making process, and how the choices we make can affect those decisions. When you Practice Choice-less Awareness, you won't need to make a decision or choose the way (it already exists) - all you have to do is recognize it. "Choice-less Awareness" is about complete awareness of what is going on within and around you without judgment or comparing it with past experience. When I use the term Choice-less Awareness, I am not suggesting that there is never an occasion for making choices since we make 100s of choices every day. What I am suggesting is that, when there is a critical decision to be made, you won't need to make a choice because you will be so consciously aware of what's going on within and around you that the decision, direction or solution will often be self-evident.

Choice-less Awareness is an objective, child-like way of looking at the world anew without judgment. To illustrate, if you are a woman, going on a date with someone you have never met, strive to see him as he really is without the emotional baggage of comparing and contrasting him with the men you have dated in the past. It's the ability to recognize him for whom or what he is, instead of whom you think he is or might want him to be.

The same holds true when you seek a sense of direction. When striving to attain a clear sense of direction, keep an open mind by not allowing your previous experience to dictate your future direction. I'm not suggesting that what you've learned from previous experience has no merit. What I am suggesting is that your previous experience can taint the decision-making process and prevent you from seeing clearly someone or something in the here and now.

It has been my experience that when I attempt to make a choice about which decision to make or direction to take, I have to deal with The Perils and Pitfalls of Choice. This often creates a great deal of stress and uncertainty about whether or not I have made the right decision or determined the right direction. However, when I pay attention to my Inner Voice, and practice Choice-less Awareness, the path or course of action always presents itself, and all I have to do is recognize it. I am confident and certain I have made the right decision, even if in the short term that path seems questionable, implausible or even illogical. Practicing Choice-less Awareness is the absence of struggle - you won't have to analyze your options, wrestle with the various directions or be racked by indecision because the "absolute certainty" of your path or course of action will be clear and self-evident. If it is not *clear and self-evident,* it's probably not the right decision, direction or course of action.

As you become adept at utilizing The Recognition Factor, you will begin to rely more on the guidance God is providing via your Inner Voice and less on the choice-making process. The reason this is critical is that the choice-making process can be fraught with potential hazards. The purpose of ACTION ITEM #4 is to introduce the Perils & Pitfalls of Choice. This is not to dismiss outright the choice-making process, since we make hundreds of choices every day, but to understand how the choice-making process can make it difficult to make the right decision about which direction to turn or path to take.

The Perils & Pitfalls of Choice

We are confident we have free agency - the free will to make a decision or choose a direction they think best. Unfortunately, we sometimes make a decision or choose a path that leads us in the wrong direction. I am not suggesting that there is no such thing as free will. I am merely saying that our will is *free* only to the extent that we don't get in our own way.

The first concern I have with the choice-making process occurs when one avoids making a decision due to the sheer magnitude of the choices available. From shampoo to clothes, from music to cars, the thousands of options available from which we have to choose can cripple the decision-making process. With so many choices available, it's easy to get overwhelmed and defer making a decision. If you choose not to make a decision, in actuality that *is* a decision because what you have decided is to take no action. In the words of Harvard Divinity scholar, Harvey Cox, "Not to decide is to decide."

If you use your free will to justify delaying a particular decision in order to examine every conceivable option, you could spend a lifetime justifying your pursuit of every potential marriage companion, career or spiritual path. When this is the case, you might not be aware that you are falling into the shopping-my-options trap in order to procrastinate or avoid indefinitely making a decision. The problem this creates is that at some point in your future, you will grow weary of all this procrastination, and wind up settling for the next relationship, job or spiritual path that presents itself, which might or might not be the right decision or direction.

The second concern I have with the choice-making process is that we frequently create the situation, context or arena in which our choices exist, only to find ourselves going in the wrong direction. Although Western culture values the concept of individual free agency, in reality our freedom of choice can be limited because of a context, arena or situation *we* choose to create, e.g. the environment in which we choose to work, the marriage partner with whom we choose to live, the church we choose to join or the direction we choose to follow. To illustrate, let's say that a friend of mine accepts my invitation to join me for lunch at a Mexican food restaurant. I could tell her that she has her free agency" and she is free to choose anything she wants from the menu. However, if it's Italian food that she wants (or needs), she would be out of luck because there are no Italian foods listed on the menu. In other words, her freedom of choice would be limited to the foods on that particular menu; a menu derived from the context or arena *we* created by choosing to go to that particular restaurant.

The third concern I have with the choice-making process is that we sometimes use our free will to make a decision that doesn't support one's Flash Point Experiment. I say this because psychologists have demonstrated that individuals tend to avoid choosing a path or direction they perceive will bring them pain or discomfort. Instead, they choose a path they think will bring the greatest pleasure or the most comfort. The reality is that the path or course of action that is most essential for you to follow could very well result in pain or discomfort, but what difference would this make if this experience facilitates your efforts to attain a clear sense of direction.

Speaking of pain or pleasure and the choice-making process, in my seminars I sometimes ask the participants to pretend I am a magician and I can make one of two things happen. The first thing I could make happen would be for them to win the lottery. The second thing I could make happen would be for them to be in a serious car wreck - one in which their car is totaled and they are injured seriously enough to require hospitalization. I then ask if they had to choose between one of these two options, which option they would choose. When I do, virtually 100% of the audience will choose to win the lottery. If I had been given these same two options before my Experiment in Living Deliberately, I too would have chosen the lottery. However, today, my response would be, *Whether the car wreck or the lottery, bring it on.* The reason for this response is that I am the one who "invited" this lesson into my life, and what I truly long for is the lesson from the Classroom that God knows is most essential for meeting my needs - COME WHAT MAY. From having the car wreck, I might learn to better value life. From winning the lottery, I might learn the limitations of what money can buy.

The final concern I have with the choice-making process is one of *perception* - the beliefs, values and ideas one has about life influences the choices they make. These beliefs, values and ideas come from their cultural conditioning and their authority figures, as well as from educational and religious institutions, and have shaped their Worldview. Consequently, their perception of which options are right, good and acceptable, or wrong, bad or unacceptable has been greatly influenced by the cultural relativism of the society in which you live. For instance, if the culture in which you choose to live dictates that eating pork is taboo, this in fact will limit your choice of meats to eat. You would not actually be *"free"* to eat pork. One more example, if the religion you have chosen prohibits interfaith marriage, gay marriage or marrying outside your caste, this will significantly influence your free will and affect your decision of about whom to marry. I'm not suggesting that this is necessarily a bad thing, but just something to keep in mind when you think you are being objective about any given decision.

SUMMARY

IV. PAY ATTENTION: *Pay conscious attention to what is going on within and around you in order to recognize the path or course of action that can provide the direction and experience necessary to meet your needs, solve your problems and fulfill your purpose.*

Step 4 introduces the 2nd component of the **Third Theme of Primessentialism**, which is to establish a sense of DIRECTION. A sense of direction is the 2nd prerequisite necessary for making your life complete. Without a sense of direction, you will find yourself wasting an enormous amount of time and energy pursuing any path or lifestyle but the one that meets your real needs. As mentioned throughout this book, the path you are seeking is the one that will provide the ideas, knowledge and experience you need to attain personal growth, spiritual development and physical well-being. These three will provide the ideas, means and tools you need to meet your needs, solve your problems and fulfill your purpose.

The "How?" question we asked at the beginning of this chapter was, *How do I determine which path or course of action will provide the life lessons and experience necessary to attain personal growth, spiritual development and physical well-being?* The answer is simply to pay conscious attention to what is going on within and around you by improving your sensory perception skills, tuning-in to your Inner Voice and practicing Choice-less Awareness.

The most important lesson I have learned from implementing Step 4 is that the *recognition of what is* (the path, direction or course of action I need to pursue) brings the *understanding of what needs to be* (why this particular path or course of action will provide the experience I need). As you "Cultivate the Recognition Factor," you will be less dependent on the choice-making process because the best decision will often be self-evident. I have also learned that the reasons many individuals pay so little attention to what is going on within and around them is because they are either living their lives on Automatic Pilot, don't trust their Inner Voice, or they lack the faith, trust and confidence necessary to seek guidance and direction from God.

With this chapter, you now have a sense of PURPOSE and the means to determine as sense of DIRECTION. In Chapter 5 you will learn the value of grasping the significance of the experience, solutions, life lessons and relationships that come with this path in order to attain a sense of MEANING.

Step #5: Embrace the Experience

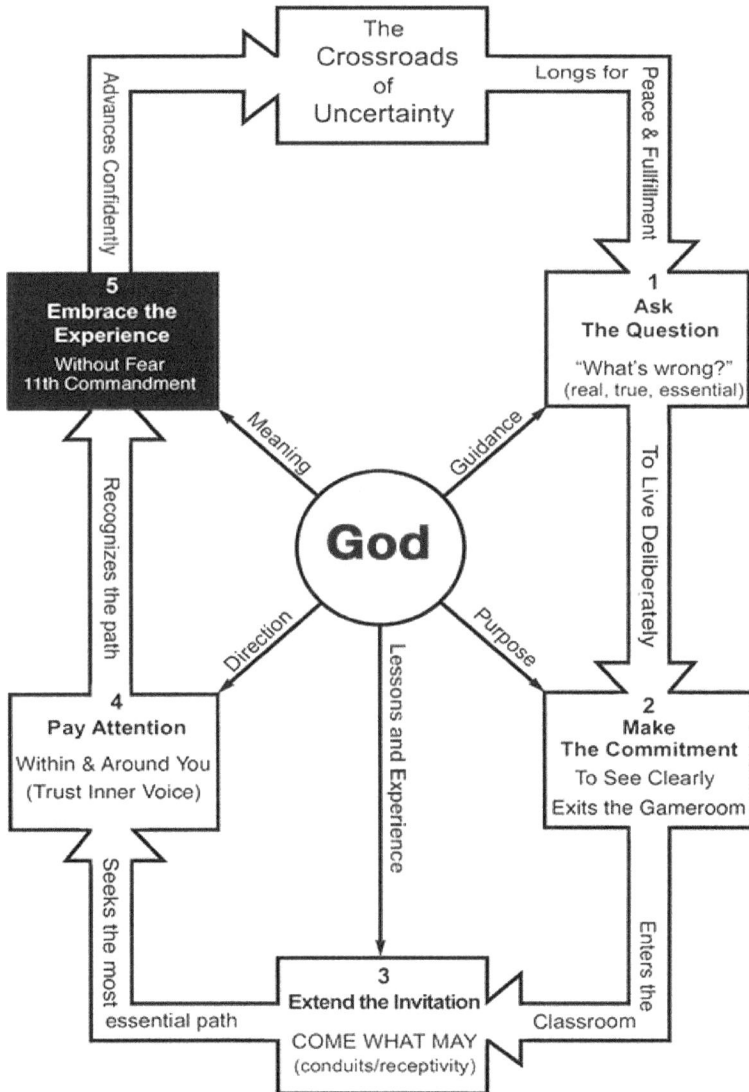

The Crossroads of Uncertainty

Advances Confidently

Longs for

Peace & Fulfillment

5
Embrace the Experience
Without Fear
11th Commandment

1
Ask
The Question
"What's wrong?"
(real, true, essential)

Meaning

Guidance

To Live Deliberately

God

Recognizes the path

4
Pay Attention
Within & Around You
(Trust Inner Voice)

Direction

Purpose

Lessons and Experience

2
Make
The Commitment
To See Clearly
Exits the Gameroom

Seeks the most
essential path

3
Extend the Invitation
COME WHAT MAY
(conduits/receptivity)

Enters the
Classroom

Chapter 5

Step Five: Embrace the Experience

EMBRACE THE EXPERIENCE - *Welcome and embrace the ideas, relationships, challenges and solutions that have come with your particular path in order to gain the insight and understanding necessary to attain a sense of meaning.* Embracing your experience creates a Flash Point - the moment at which you understand the significance of any particular lesson, relationship or experience, and what it has come to teach you. This sense of MEANING, coupled with a clear sense of PURPOSE and DIRECTION, will make your life complete.

"Whatever good or bad fortune may come our way we can always give it meaning and transform it into something of value." Hermann Hesse, *Siddhartha*

A. WHY EMBRACE THE EXPERIENCE?

- Primarily because you now have a measure of balance, as well as a sense of Purpose and Direction, and you long for the sense of Meaning necessary to make your life complete.

- Because you long to make sense of your life experience. This is crucial because anytime you are experiencing a relationship, career or spiritual path that is meaningless, there will be a void of Peace & Fulfillment in your life.

- Because your current experience is who and what you have invited into your life, either subconsciously or consciously. To deny this reality is to shirk responsibility for your current circumstances or station in life, which only perpetuates The Cycle of Discontent.

- Because you want to understand why some of the lessons and experiences coming from God's Classroom without Walls continue to repeat themselves.

- Because the nature and quality of your life experience is what it is, and many of your fears and much of your disillusionment come from wanting your life to be something, anything other than what it currently is.

When you embrace your experience, you're acknowledging that you are weary from living with fear, worry and uncertainty, all of which reflect a lack of meaning in your life. In addition, you are eager to learn *why* any particular life lesson or relationship experience has come with your path, as well as *how* this experience will meet your needs, solve your problems and fulfill your purpose. As your life becomes more balanced and complete, you want to know how you can sustain this sense of Peace & Fulfillment from one crossroads in life to the next.

B. MY EXPERIENCE - Once I invited God to send the lessons and experience for meeting my needs (Step 3) and recognized at least some of the path(s) that would provide those lessons and that experience (Step 4), I now had a sense of PURPOSE and DIRECTION, but still lacked a sense of MEANING. As I continued to pursue these paths, I began to encounter a number of lessons and experiences from the Classroom that were difficult for me to grasp their significance for my life.

These experiences were difficult because they challenged me to confront some of my deepest fears, acknowledge many of my shortcomings, and face the reality of my then current beliefs and lifestyle. At first, I tried to ignore or avoid many of the lessons God was trying to teach me. What experience I could not avoid, I tried to manipulate or control to match my version of how things should be. As time passed, the sheer volume of things and relations that I was trying to control became increasingly problematic and difficult to juggle.

I finally reached a point where I didn't want to keep repeating this Cycle of Discontent. I decided that if I were going to bring any sense of meaning to my life experience, I would need to quit trying to control this experience and start trying to understand why I continued to bring this experience into being. I decided to stop ignoring the lessons and solutions that were coming from God's Classroom without Walls and start practicing the acceptance necessary to gain this understanding. In addition, I needed to find a way to overcome the fears and uncertainties that were preventing me from embracing these lessons and solutions.

At that same time, I was also struggling to determine how much accountability and responsibility I should accept for the Train Wreck I had made of my life. My first move was to blame others or make excuses for my misfortunes. However, after I began my Flash Point Experiment, I realized I couldn't blame anyone else. After all, I was the one who had Extended the Invitation that had brought this experience, and its resulting Train Wreck, into being.

The "How?" question I needed to answer was, *How do I gain the insight necessary to understand the significance of the lessons, ideas, and solutions that have come with my path?*

C. THE MAIN IDEAS – Now that you have moved toward establishing a sense of PURPOSE and DIRECTION, the final step toward making your life complete is to establish a sense of MEANING. Have you ever asked yourself, *What is the meaning of life?* It's not the purpose of this chapter to serve as some kind of oracle that sets forth a universal or profound meaning of life. The purpose is to help you answer this question by providing the tools necessary to make sense of your life; to understand the significance of the life lessons, people and circumstances that have come with your particular path. Subsequently, Step 5 is primarily about meaning and sustainability. A sense of MEANING is the 3rd component of the **Third Theme of**

Primessentialism, and sustainability is about how to advance confidently from one crossroads in life to the next. When you couple this sense of meaning with a sense of purpose and direction, you gain the insight and understanding that makes your life whole or complete - which is the **Fourth Theme of Primessentialism**. When I say, complete, I *don't* mean that there is nothing left to add to your life, I mean there is nothing essential that is missing in your life.

As you continue to expand your personal growth, spiritual development and physical well-being and have established a sense of purpose, direction and meaning, all your basic and higher needs will be met, and your life will be complete. Anything above or beyond these needs might be desirable to attain, achieve or accumulate, but these are not essential for making your life complete.

When I use the word, "expand," I mean that the Flash Point Process is a continually evolving process, not a destination. Ideally, you will continue to add to your personal growth, spiritual development and physical well-being all the days of your life.

Step 4 was about bringing into being a sense of direction by recognizing the path or course of action that would provide the life lessons and relationships experiences necessary to meet your needs. However, in order to gain the insight necessary to make sense of your experience, it's not enough to merely recognize this path. The principle objective of Step 5 is to encourage you to love and embrace *all* the ideas, life lessons, relationships, experiences and solutions that come with your particular path in order to understand what they have come to teach you. I've learned that, when I view any life lesson or experience as meaningless, what I am really saying is that I have yet to grasp the significance of that experience; what it has come to teach me.

There are thousands of books written to address the question, *What is the meaning of life?* You would think that such a universal question wouldn't be that difficult to answer. Quite the contrary, the before-mentioned Barna Group Poll revealed that 86% of the American population have no sense of meaning in their lives. I think that some of the reasons this question is difficult to answer is because meaning varies from person to person and can change over time and under different circumstances. In addition, what was meaningful to you in your youth might not be meaningful to you as an adult.

I say this because meaning is not an inherent quality of some relationship, thing, experience or event, because the meaning of anything is simply the value or significance the individual assigns to it. For example, the American dollar bill is just a piece of cotton paper with a material worth of less than two cents, but the value we have assigned it is one dollar. Another example, the cash value of my wedding ring is about $1,000, but I would not take $2,000 for it because of the significance it holds in my life. One last example: two different people can hear the same lecture or sermon - to one it is very meaningful, but to the other it is meaningless, depending on the value they assign to it. It's not the purpose of this course of instruction to assign a specific meaning to your life experience. This is something only you can establish. However, it can provide you with the tools to determine for yourself the significance of the relationships, experiences and life lessons that come with your path.

Pardon the pun, but the word *meaning* has many different meanings. For the purposes of the Flash Point Process, I use Merriam-

Webster's definition: "What is intended to be; the significance of something."

Establishing a sense of MEANING is the 3rd and final Prerequisite for making your life complete. Without meaning, you won't understand the *significance* of the lessons and experiences that have come with your path or why this particular lesson or experience needs *to be* in your life. There can be no certainty without this understanding because without this insight, life becomes confusing, frustrating and meaningless, and a meaningless life will never be complete.

Establishing a Sense of Meaning

Why is meaning so critical to Living Deliberately? I would suggest that it is only through meaning that we can internalize, interpret, evaluate and make sense of the life lessons, relationships and experiences that comes with our paths. When life makes sense, there is peace, certainty, hope and contentment. When life doesn't make sense there is fear, disillusionment, uncertainty and discontent. In addition, it is through meaning that we find ways to meet our needs and solve our problems, because when you understand what something means, the solution will be more self-evident.

In his book, *Man's Search for Meaning,* the psychiatrist Viktor E. Frankl observed that man's search for meaning is the primary motivation in life and "…a firm sense of meaning is essential for optimal human development." In this book, he recounts his experience in a Nazi concentration camp during World War II. When the allies liberated the camp toward the end of the war, Frankl observed that many of the men who survived were those who had a specific reason to continue living. They had a reason for staying alive, a sense of meaning in their life, e.g. a family to go home to, a book to write, a career to which to return, etc. Those prisoners, whose lives were void of meaning tended to give up hope, stopped struggling to survive and didn't live to see their camp liberated. You will probably never find yourself captive in a concentration camp, but without a sense of meaning, life can become so senseless that you give up, and become captive to fear, uncertainty, depression and hopelessness.

This chapter will facilitate your efforts to discover the sense of meaning necessary to make your life complete by introducing the following:

- How life's lessons have a way of repeating themselves until you grasp their significance (WHAT I'VE LEARNED).
- The value of accepting your share of responsibility for the nature and quality of your experience (THE QUESTION).
- How embracing your life experience will add a sense of meaning to that experience (ACTION ITEMS #1).
- How to manage any fears that could be preventing you from attaining a sustainable of Peace & Fulfillment ACTION ITEM #2).
- The value of giving up the need to control (ACTION ITEM #3).
- The 4 Keys for sustaining your resolve to advance confidently from one crossroads in life to the next (ACTION ITEM #4).

D. WHAT I'VE LEARNED - *My most essential experience is relentless and progressive. It continually unfolds and returns in one form or another, increasing in intensity and frequency until I embrace it.* "If it is time to learn a specific lesson, then events will happen that set up the perfect opportunity. If the lesson isn't heeded, then another set of events will occur that offer the same lesson." Gloria Karpinski, *Where Two Worlds Touch*

There is a biography of Jim Morrison, the lead singer of the 60s rock band The Doors, that is titled *No One Here Gets Out Alive*. In a similar sense, this **5th Primessential Principle** suggests that no one gets out of life without experiencing the lessons they need from God's Classroom without Walls. In other words, the life lessons and experience you need to make your life complete, will continue to recur until you learn what these lessons mean to you. Any given lesson might remain the same, but its content and form might change over time. For example, let's say that with your first marriage, you married someone who was physically abusive. With your second marriage, you married a man who was culturally, physically and intellectually the exact opposite of your first spouse. However, in time he also reveals himself physically abusive. My point being that, in the theater of your life, the actors changed, but the script remained the same. In order to glean any sense of meaning from your life experience, you might consider to stop dating until you come to grips with why you continue to attract this particular kind of experience into your life.

You have possibly met individuals who appear to make the same mistakes over-and-over again throughout the course of their lives, e.g. one failed relationship or marriage after another, continuously in financial straits or constantly changing jobs. It's been my observation that, over time, each failure tends to become increasingly problematic until you understand what it has come to teach you. Of course, there is nothing wrong with making mistakes since this is part of Personal Growth. A problem arises when we fail to learn from our mistakes. I've learned that, when I repeatedly make the same mistake it is no longer simply a mistake, but actually a choice or habit.

I think one reason that people have difficulty breaking this mistake habit is that they don't know *how* to do things differently. They don't want to keep repeating the same mistakes, but they simply lack the knowledge, experience or example necessary to do things differently. For example, you could take the case of a child who grew up in a broken home or dysfunctional family where there was physical, sexual or emotional abuse, alcohol or drug abuse, or there was an absence of love, affection and nurturing. When this child becomes an adult, he will experience one failed relationship after another because he doesn't have an example of what constitutes a normal, healthy relationship so he doesn't know how to have such a relationship.

Another reason people keep repeating these "mistake habits" is because they don't understand *why* the lessons from the Classroom continue to repeat themselves. Consequently, they tend to ignore, ovoid or postpone the very lessons they need. When I was teaching college, most courses utilized an A, B, C, D grading system, while others used a pass/fail system. A pass/fail course is one you have to keep repeating until you pass it because you cannot graduate without it. The Classroom without Walls utilizes the pass/fail system. Sometimes the lessons Will be obvious and easy to grasp, while others will require a great deal of introspection and reflection. If you continue to ignore these lessons, you will keep repeating the same life mistakes until you encounter a series of Big Thumpers that will increase in frequency and intensity until that particular experience has your full attention.

This chapter will suggest ways to stop repeating the same lessons by encouraging you to accept responsibility for your current situation and circumstances, and stop trying to manipulate and control the people and events in your life. Instead, it will encourage you to embrace those relationships and events, in order to glean a sense of meaning from that experience.

E. THE QUESTION - *Why am I trying to avoid this experience if I'm the one responsible for bringing it into being?* - "You think me the child of my circumstances: I make my circumstances." Ralph Waldo Emerson, *Essays*

Are you ready to accept a reasonable degree of accountability and responsibility for the experiences, circumstances and relationships that are, or are not, currently in your life? It is a key concept of Primessentialism that once you launch your Flash Point Experiment, you are directly or indirectly responsible for the bulk of whom or what is, or is not, in your life, as well as your current circumstances and station in life. If this were not the case, then you would be someone else, experiencing something else.

I acknowledge that there is an element of randomness, luck and timing to life, and there are circumstances that are beyond my control. However, I have learned that most of whom or what I experience on a daily basis is someone or something for which I have subconsciously or consciously longed to bring into being. I repeat:

The majority of whom and what I experience in my daily life is either the result of a subconscious decision, driven by my Checklist of Wants & Desires, or a conscious decision, driven by my having Extended the Invitation.

In other words, once you have honestly and sincerely invited God to send the life lessons and experience you need (COME WHAT MAY) you will need to accept responsibility for the nature of this life and the quality of that experience. It's been my observation that many of our seminar participants try to avoid the very lessons and circumstances necessary to make their lives more complete because they believe that they are the victim and not the source of those circumstances. In other words, they often go throughout their days thinking that life is something that just happens to them. They believe that they are not directly or even indirectly responsible for bringing into being the life lessons, relationships, and circumstances they encounter on a daily basis.

This victim mentality can prevent you from gleaning any meaning from your life experience. When you refuse to accept responsibility for your current station in life, it might provide you with some self-justifying excuses, e.g. the Blame Game or Victim Game. In addition, it might give you something to do - like senseless worry. However, blaming others or senseless worry serve absolutely no purpose and can prevent you from gleaning any sense of meaning from your life's challenges. On the other hand, when you accept personal responsibility for your experience you will gain the insight and understanding to lend meaning to that experience.

- When you marry, you accept your share of responsibility for supporting this union. As you do, it lends meaning to your life (a sense of love, unity, intimacy and companionship).
- When you have a child, you accept responsibility for the upbringing of that child, and this in turn lends new meaning to your life (a sense of family, completeness and fulfillment).
- As you accept responsibility for your current employment or unemployment situation, it adds meaning to your life (being in charge of your destiny).
- When you accept responsibility for the lessons and experience you have invited from the Classroom, it adds meaning to your life (a closer relationship with God and a sense of ownership of your life experience)

F. THE ACTION ITEMS – "One cannot live without meaning." Albert Camus, French philosopher

Onc way to understand the significance of your life lessons and experience is to think of life, not as a competitive game to play, but more like a jigsaw picture puzzle to solve. Each piece of this puzzle represents some aspect of life that is necessary to lend meaning to your picture, e.g. relationships, career, education, health, finances, self-awareness and spirituality.

The ACTION ITEMS in this step will facilitate your efforts to embrace and reflect on the life lessons and experience that comes with each piece of your "puzzle" so you can better understand how each piece fits into the bigger picture – its significance. Once you grasp the significance of any given puzzle piece, you will see how it contributes to solving your puzzle, meeting your needs and fulfilling your purpose. In order to complete your picture, you will need to accept that it is *your* puzzle to solve. Therefore, it will be necessary to let go of your fear of your life picture not turning out like it is supposed to (or as others think it should) and stop trying to force into place those pieces that don't fit by giving up control. I might add that one of the challenges to solving this puzzle is that the puzzle pieces come in a box without a photo of the completed picture. You alone will determine how the final picture will look – interesting, compelling and meaningful or disappointing, incomplete and meaningless.

The first three ACTION ITEMS in Step 5 will facilitate your efforts to attain a sense of meaning by demonstrating the value of loving, embracing and accepting responsibility for your life experience. The 4th ACTION ITEM will provide you with the tools necessary to sustain your sense of Peace & Fulfillment as your life journey takes you from one

Crossroads in life to the next.

ACTION ITEM #1: Embrace Your Experience - "A simple acceptance of what comes to us, regard it as neither bad nor good." Friedrich Nietzsche

Throughout this course of instruction, you have made the deliberate effort to find the path that will provide the lessons and experiences necessary to meet your basic and higher needs as well as solve your problems. However, if you fail to embrace the lessons, experience, people, circumstances and solutions that come with this path, you will not attain the sense of meaning necessary to make your life complete. The purpose of ACTION ITEM #1 is to demonstrate the value of, and provide examples of, ways to embrace the lessons and experience that come with your path in order to determine their significance in your life. I have deliberately used the phrase, "Embrace Your Experience," instead of just enduring or resigning yourself to that experience. The word *embrace* implies the enthusiastic, joyful welcoming of *all* the experience that comes with your path, *regardless* of the nature of that experience.

To Embrace Your Experience requires the uncompromising integrity to accept not only responsibility for the nature and quality of your life experience, but also to strive to understand the lessons behind that that experience. As you gain insight and understanding, you will experience a series of Flash Points. Those "Ah ha!" moments that will enable you to grasp the significance of any given life lesson or experience that has come with your path, and how this experience will meet your needs, solve your problems and complete your picture:

- Perhaps a relationship has come to teach about you love, intimacy, companionship, compromise, trust or loyalty.

- Maybe an idea has come to meet your needs or solve your problems.

- A life crisis might have come to challenge you to question your secular, moral or religious beliefs.

- Perhaps a challenging or difficult experience has come to teach patience or introspection.

When you embrace these lessons and experiences, this will bring the insight and understanding necessary to attain a sense of meaning. Without this understanding, your picture will remain unclear and incomplete at best - or at worst it will look like someone else's picture.

We ultimately attract or bring into being the life lessons, relationships, events and experience prioritized on our Checklist of Wants & Desires. This is often referred to as, "The Law of Attraction." This is to say, we generally attract who or what we expect to experience, e.g. uptight people experience an uptight world, drama queens experience a world filled with chaos, individuals playing the Victim Game experience a world of persecution. Individuals who view life as a competitive game ultimately realize that The Game of Life, like all games, is in essence a game of chance, luck and timing. The oddsmakers in Las Vegas have proven that when you play a game of chance, you will lose more often that you will win. "I attract to my life whatever I give my attention energy and focus to , whether positive or negative." Michael Losier, author of *Law of Attraction*

Considering this dynamic of attraction, it's no wonder so few people willingly embrace their life experience, because historically the experience they attract is often the result of their trying to live up to someone else's version of their life. Subsequently, the lessons and experiences they attract will only meet someone else's needs, but not their own, so they remain trapped in The Cycle of Discontent.

When you find yourself thinking, *anywhere, anyone or anything but this,* remember that you are the one who invited this life lesson or experience into your life – COME WHAT MAY. To long for someone else's experience is to miss the very experience you need to make sense of your life. For instance, if you have a history of financial instability, you might long to have what the rich man has - which is financial security. However, if you have not learned *why* you are always plagued with financial difficulties, and you do manage to come into some money, your history has demonstrated that this will also mismanage this money. This lesson will continue to repeat itself until you understand *why* you keep making this particular mistake.

Another way to Embrace Your Experience is to think, WIN/WIN - an acronym for *Whatever Is Necessary/Whatever Is Needed.* Whomever or whatever you are experiencing, if it is in your life today, there is something for you to learn from it. Whether your path brings heartache and frustration or joy and happiness, don't ignore or run away from that experience. Whether your experience is positive or negative, embrace it by showing gratitude for the lesson, or opportunity at hand by thanking God for this experience. *Thank you God for this experience, whatever is necessary, whatever is needed at this stage of my life.*

One last way to embrace your experience is not to view your life experience in terms of *good* or *bad* but strive to see everything and everyone in your life as an *interesting* lesson from the Classroom. When your experience is pleasurable, positive or smooth think, *Ah, this experience is so rewarding, it's interesting.* When your experience is hurtful, negative or frustrating, think, *Ah, this experience is so challenging, it's interesting.* When you embrace your experience, you will always find life to be interesting and meaningful, instead of dull and meaningless. In order to gain a greater understanding of any particular life lesson or experience, ask questions like:

- What's the significance of this experience - what has this person, life lesson or situation come to teach me?
- Why do these kinds of situations and relationships keep reappearing on my journey through life?
- Why is the solution that came with my Invitation so difficult for me to accept?
- What is this relationship or experience telling me that I need to examine - is it my personality, thoughts, beliefs or actions?
- Why am I so dissatisfied with my relationship, career or spiritual path when I am the one who extended the invitation that brought this path into being?

ACTION ITEM #1 is the most challenging of the four

ACTION ITEMS, because in order to attain a clear sense of meaning, it will be necessary to embrace everyone and everything you encounter on a daily basis. When I say everything, I mean EVERYTHING, regardless what the day may bring. When your life or relationship experience is interesting, easy or pleasant then embracing it is not that difficult. However, when this experience is uncomfortable, unpleasant or frustrating it can be very difficult to accept, much less embrace. For instance, good health or financial stability are easy to embrace, whereas sickness and indebtedness are not so easy to embrace. Nonetheless, *both* kinds of experiences might be necessary for your personal growth, spiritual development and physical well-being, and they need to be embraced equally. If you try to avoid or asked to be excused from any given life experience it will continue to press you until you face it, embrace it and deal with it. As you strive to embrace your experience, it will be necessary to set aside, or at least learn to manage, any fears that could be blocking your ability to understand the significance of the lesson behind that experience.

F. ACTION ITEM #2: Set Aside Your fears - "Fear is the brain's way of saying that there is something important for you to overcome." Rachel Huber, American writer

Earlier we talked about exercising courage in the face of fear. The purpose of ACTION ITEM #2 is to provide you with the skills necessary to examine the legitimacy and significance of any fears that are preventing you from embracing your experience. Consequently, this ACTION ITEM will provide you with some practical tools to help you manage more effectively those fears.

As you encounter new relationships and experiences on your path, be mindful that any fears you might have could prevent you from gleaning any sense of meaning from this experience. I say this because your fear and uncertainty can cause you to cling to whomever or whatever is known and familiar rather than embrace a lesson or relationship experience from the Classroom that might be unknown or unfamiliar. In the words of Naguib Mahfouz, "Fear does not prevent death, it prevents life." Please note that I said "manage your fears," not eliminate them. I say this because fear can be very tenacious – existing fears you will learn to set aside, but new fears will continue to pop up. The objective is not to try and eliminate your fears because fear is part of the human condition. The objective is to move through life in spite of any given fear.

It wasn't until I began my Flash Point Experiment that I started becoming truly fearless by striving to love and embrace my life experience, and not wanting this experience to be anything other than what it was. It was at that point that I realized that when I allow fear to take over my life, I need to remind myself that I invited this circumstance, lesson or relationship into my life – COME WHAT MAY. Therefore, I need to embrace that experience, and not run away from it, *regardless* of the nature of that experience. I've learned that,

The basis of all fear, disillusionment and discontent is the result of wanting any given life lesson, situation or relationship to be

anything other than what it actually is.

The dictionary defines fear as, "An unpleasant emotion caused by the belief that someone or something is dangerous; likely to cause pain or a threat." When it comes to managing fear, the operative word in this definition is *belief.* Fear is not something that forces itself on us; we allow fear to take hold of us. It's an internal belief; it's a perception, but not necessarily a reality. For example, a young child might believe there are monsters under his bed, and this belief generates his fear. However, this is just his belief, not a actual reality. A life free from unwarranted fear, worry and uncertainty is essentially a decision. It's a decision to examine the significance of those fears to see if they are grounded in reality, and actually pose a threat, or they are merely a belief.

I should also mention that, sometimes fear comes from a lack of confidence. The reality is that you are still alive today in spite of the worries, fears and uncertainties you faced last year, last month, last week or yesterday. Once you acknowledge to yourself that you have in fact been able to survive life in spite of your past fears, you will begin breaking the fear habit, and have the increased confidence that you can manage any future fears. In the words of William Allen White, "I am not afraid of tomorrow, for I have seen yesterday and I love today."

I think it is ok to be afraid every now and then since there will be times when we will all face uncertainty or the unknown. Therefore, it's useful to have some proven tools for managing those fears. In order to manage better your fears, realize that the thing feared is truly a danger and movement or change is necessary, or that fear is an unwarranted belief, and that belief needs to be questioned, challenged or set aside. To facilitate your efforts to manage your fears, utilize the 3 Keys for

Managing Fear:

3 Keys for Managing Fear

1. **Examine Their Reality**
2. **Consider Your Options**
3. **Determine Their Probability**

1. Examine Their Reality - Real danger is a fact not just a belief. The fear of fire, fear of drowning, fear of poisonous snakes, etc. are all warranted fears. However, the majority of our fears are irrational and unwarranted because sociologists have demonstrated that babies have only two natural fears: the fear of falling and the fear of loud noises. All other fears we acquire through personal experience or inherit from our cultural conditioning. The kinds of fears I am talking about are those that are unwarranted. Some examples of unwarranted fears could include:

- Fear of failure
- Fear of being alone
- Fear of making a mistake
- Fear of intimacy
- Fear of the unknown
- Fear of change
- Fear of rejection
- Fear of success
- Fear of knowing God's Will for your life

As mentioned earlier, you alone will decide what you allow yourself to feel about anything, and this includes feelings of fear. Bear in mind, that every minute you choose to have feelings of fear, is a moment you *choose* to push peace and joy out of your life. I've learned that, people who have faith, trust and confidence in God have significantly fewer fears or worries than those who don't; the greater the faith, the less the fear. "Fear thou not, for I am with thee." Isaiah 41:10

Danger is real, but the feeling of fear is a choice. The unwarranted fears you choose to cling to can hamper your Flash Point Experiment, and cripple your efforts to glean any sense of meaning from the experience or situation that is triggering that fear. Are your fears warranted or unwarranted? It's important to remember that beliefs are not necessarily reality. When facing a problem, avoid irrational or exaggerated language because this can generate fear. For example, when you believe that you will never find the career that's right for you, ask yourself if this is warranted or just what you believe at this point? Do you fear you will *never* find that career, or do you simply mean that it is not readily apparent?

We have been culturally conditioned to believe that we are not supposed to be at peace when faced with any given fear, but this is a myth. This myth is not reality because neither your worry and uncertainty nor your fear accomplishes anything. They won't change your circumstances or solve your problems. Fear and worry will do nothing to provide you with a meaningful life or healthy relationship. Fear never provides clarity or meaning - it only cripples activity. To embrace your experience is proactive, to fear your experience is reactive.

I've learned that, the same mind that can generate thoughts of fear is the same mind that can generate thoughts of peace and happiness. It's simply my choice as to which thoughts I will allow to support or hinder my Flash Point Experiment.

Be patient with your efforts to overcome your fears because many of them have accrued over a lifetime; with some originating all the way back to childhood. When you cling to your fears over a long period of time, they can become a fear habit. Like any habit, it takes time to break and become truly fearless, but this habit can often be broken with simply a new perspective or more accurate knowledge. When faced with a fear-inducing situation or problem, we tend to worry about or around the problem, but not actually think about the reality of the problem itself.

Sometimes what's needed is simply a different perspective about that problem. For example, when you experience a painful breakup with your significant other or go through a difficult divorce, you might be fearful that you will never again be able to find love again. When this is your belief, and you don't quickly find another companion, there is a high probability that you will allow yourself to feel uncertainty, worry or fear. Instead, when you lose that significant other, and you changed your perspective to, *I'm ready for a new and more fulfilling relationship.* This new perspective would provide a different, positive reality and open up all kinds of new possibilities. Possibilities you might not have considered if you allowed yourself to wallow in self-pity or allow your fears to cloud your thinking. Every time you start experiencing feelings of fear, worry or self-pity, simply say to yourself, "I could see peace instead of this." From the book, *A Course in Miracles*

2. Consider Your Options – Another way to manage your fears is to ask yourself if there are other options you should consider. Instead of being afraid of choosing the wrong career, companion or spiritual path, ask yourself if there are options to your fear. When considering my options, I utilize what I refer to as the "Helen Keller Factor.

The Helen Keller Factor

Helen Keller, although she was stricken blind and deaf in her infancy, she went on to have a remarkable career, wrote a book, starred in movies, and overcame enormous obstacles. She once made the following observation, "Although it is true the world is full of suffering, it is equally true that the world is full of the overcoming of suffering." Therefore, the model for the Helen Keller Factor is as follows:

Although it is true that _____, it is equally true that _____.

For example, if you are having difficulty finding companionship you could apply the Helen Keller Factor by saying to yourself, *Although it is true I am having difficulty finding a meaningful relationship, it is equally true that there is someone for everyone and with patience I will find my someone.* If you have failed at something, you could say to yourself, *Although it is true that I have been weak and strayed (from my diet, my spouse, my spiritual path, etc.), it is equally true that I can be strong and faithful again.* Another example, *Although it is true I don't have much formal education, it is equally true that lots of people with little formal education are highly successful in life.*

3. Determine Their Probability - Is what you fear certain, probable or merely possible? When I was a Communications Consultant with AT&T® they distributed a study involving a group of 1,100 employees that had been conducted over the course of one year to determine the probability of people's fears turning out as they had anticipated. At the beginning of the study, they asked this group to fill out a questionnaire and list their fears. At the end of the study, they completed a second questionnaire to determine if those fears were justified. Of the dire consequences feared:

- 42% never occurred
- 35% occurred as feared, but nothing could have changed the outcome
- 13% were not as bad as originally feared
- 8% occurred as feared, but had little or no effect
- 2% actually occurred as feared and had the anticipated outcome

In other words, the odds are very slim that *anything* you fear will actually occur and have the outcome you feared. When I find myself immobilized by worry or fear, I practice what I refer to as "future perfect tense." I do this by *rolling the tape forward*, i.e. I picture in my mind the future outcome I fear, and ask myself if that outcome is certain, probable or merely possible. I then ask myself, *What does this mean, what kind of action do I need to take, and is this an outcome something I should fear or embrace?* When faced with fear or uncertainty, *roll the tape forward* by projecting in your mind's eye the outcome of that which you fear. For example, if you fear not being able to find the career of your choice, ask yourself the following questions:

- Is the outcome I fear certain? *No, it's not certain, it's only how I feel right now.*
- Is it only probable? *It is probably not going to happen, so instead of worrying I could use this time to better prepare myself to further my career.*
- Is it merely possible? *Although it is possible, statistics suggest that it's highly unlikely.*

ACTION ITEM #3: Give Up Control – "Life is to be lived, not controlled." Ralph Ellison, *The Invisible Man*

In addition to our fears, the urge to manipulate and control our life experience is yet another self-imposed habit that prevents us from loving and embracing our experience. In Chapter 3, we talked about the difference between trying to *force* things to happen versus cultivating the receptivity to make or *allow* things to happen. The purpose of ACTION ITEM #3 is to provide additional insight into the futility of trying to force things to happen by trying to manipulate and control the people and events in your life. The word *control* is defined as, "The power to influence or direct people's behavior or the course of events."

The desire to control is not necessarily a bad thing. There are times when one does need to take control, like controlling one's car when driving or controlling one's budget. The most important facet of control is self-control, like controlling one's temper during an argument, controlling one's intake of food or alcohol, and controlling one's reactions when faced with fear or uncertainty. However, when you attempt to control any given life lesson, relationship or situation, it reflects a belief that who or what you are experiencing isn't fulfilling your wants and desires and needs to be controlled or manipulated in order to *force* the desired outcome. When you welcome and accept responsibility for your life experience, it reflects a belief that who or what you are experiencing is an essential lesson from the Classroom, and you need to embrace it in order to *facilitate* the necessary outcome. Exerting control in order to force a desired outcome is like trying to force a wrong puzzle piece into your picture of life. Regardless of how hard you try to *force* that career, spiritual path or relationship to work, it just won't fit or have any meaning. This puzzle will continue to frustrate you until you discover what fits - the life lesson, experience or solution that's timely and essential for completing your picture.

In the first 41 years of my life, I usually had a predetermined agenda about how things and relations were supposed to be based on my cultural conditioning, e.g. what kind of husband, friend, father, employee or church member I should be. I did my absolute best to control the relationships, circumstances and events in my life so things and relations would turn out as I thought they should. At the time, I thought this was a good thing because to me it meant I was in control. When we are afraid that life won't work out like we think it is supposed to, we often try to control as many variables as possible in order to force the desired outcome. I think this is because there is a social stigma that implies that one should never be *out of control*. However, like much of our cultural conditioning, this stigma is also a myth. I say this because, although it's possible to have a degree of control over relationships, events and situations, it is very difficult to control the outcome. "You have power over your mind-not over outside events. Realize this, and you will find strength." Marcus Aurelius, Roman Statesman

I've learned that, I can't really control relationships, circumstances or events, I can only control the manner in which I respond to those relationships, circumstances and events.

ACTION ITEM #4: Advance Confidently - "I learned this, at least, by my experiment that if one advances confidently in the direction of one's dreams, and endeavors to live the life which one has imagined, one will meet with a success unexpected in common hours." Henry David Thoreau, *Walden: Or, Life in the Woods*

As you attain a sense of purpose, direction and meaning your life will be complete, which is the **Fourth Theme of Primessentialism**. The purpose of ACTION ITEM #4 is to create a system that will enable you to sustain this sense of completeness as you progress along your path - the sustainability necessary to advance confidently from one crossroads in life to the next. This is necessary because there is no end to the number of life lessons and relationships you will have or crossroads you will face, there is no "finish line." Each time you grasp the significance of any given life lesson, experience or relationship, you will gain additional insight and understanding. This in turn will better prepare you for your next life lesson or relationship. By "insight," I mean you will begin to see clearly, the significance of the lessons, relationships and life experiences that have come with your path. By "understanding" I mean the Flash Points that will enable you to grasp *how* this particular piece of your puzzle fits into the overall scheme of things, and *why* it's needed to complete your picture, fill your void and end your longing. It is only when your life is complete that you will be prepared for, and receptive to, a sustainable measure of Peace & Fulfillment, which is the **Fifth Theme of Primessentialism**.

To Advance Confidently from one crossroads to the next, I suggest you establish a system today to help you meet the challenges of tomorrow. This will keep you from getting lost, overwhelmed or discouraged when you hit a roadblock on your journey. We could draw on the sport of archery to illustrate such a system. One way to picture this is to look at your goal to sustain your Peace & Fulfillment as your target. If you had only one arrow in your quiver (a pouch for holding arrows), the odds are fairly slim that you will actually hit this "target" unless you are very lucky or an experienced archer. However, when you have many arrows at your disposal, the odds of eventually hitting any given target greatly increase. Although there are many ways to sustain yourself on your path to Peace & Fulfillment, I suggest that the key is to have at your disposal as many arrows as possible. In order to accomplish this, add the following 4 Keys for sustainability to your system, with each key serving as one of your "arrows."

4 Keys for Sustainability

1. Keep the 11th Commandment

2. Watch Your Thoughts

3. Practice Acorn-ness

4. Never Give Up.

The 1ˢᵗ Key: Keep the 11ᵗʰ Commandment - "Above all, don't lie to yourself…the man who lies to himself can be more readily offended than anyone else." Fodor Dostoyevsky, *The Brothers Karamazov*

None of us likes to think of ourselves as someone who is living a lie. Even when we do deceive ourselves, the chances are good that we are not conscious of it because our beliefs, thoughts and habits have accumulated over the course of our lifetime. You might not be conscious of the fact that you are deceiving yourself until you reach a point in life when someone or some event brings it to your attention, e.g. a Big Thumper.

When I first began my Flash Point Experiment, I felt that, to an extent, I had been living a lie the first 40 years of my life. By this, I don't mean I was consciously trying to deceive myself or others. I just didn't want to acknowledge that I was living a life of self-deception by trying to live up to everyone's expectations. As I began my Flash Point Experiment, I realized that I was probably going to make some mistakes, but at least they would be *my* mistakes. I resolved that any failures would come by my own hand and not as the result of trying to live up to everyone else's expectations. A resolve I refer to as Keeping the 11ᵗʰ Commandment.

The 11ᵗʰ Commandment: Be True to Thy Self

What does it mean to "Keep the 11th Commandment"? I would suggest that it means heeding your Inner Voice, and trusting God, in the face of fear, uncertainty and doubt – COME WHAT MAY. Five years into my Flash Point Experiment, I decided I needed some kind of daily reminder to "be true to myself." At that point, I tried to think of a single word or phrase that would reflect all my personal philosophy (Primessentialism) as well as my thoughts, beliefs, actions and purpose. The word I chose was *righteous*. I chose this word, not in the sense of adhering to a set of religious creeds or because I believed I was even remotely close to being a righteous person. I chose this word because of its Greek root word, *alethinos*, which means, "real or genuine." With this definition in mind, I knew I needed to *keep it real* - knowing that anytime, every time, I stopped trusting my Inner Voice I would be compromising my principles, practicing self-deception and sabotaging my path to a fulfilling life, career and spiritual path. "There's something in everybody that longs for that awakening to be more true to yourself." Eckhart Tolle, *A New Earth*.

To this end, I made the word **"S.T.A.R."** (**S**tay **T**rue **A**nd **R**ighteous) a personal acronym to remind me to stay true to myself. To keep this concept in front of me, I attached tiny metal stars to some of my clothes and put a star decal on my desk and on my front door. In addition, I had a small star tattooed on my shoulder (I know, I know, tattoos are taboo for some people, but this has proved a very useful reminder for me).

Something else that has helped to remind me to be true to myself was to tell my friends and family what I was trying to accomplish with my Flash Point Experiment. You might have done something similar to this when you tried to lose weight or quit smoking. Your friends and family provided the external support you needed to attain your goal. Whenever I begin deceiving myself as to what kind of friend, husband or father I am, my friends, wife and children don't hesitate to point out any shortcomings or misconceptions I might have about myself. I should add that they have done so frequently and at times quite gleefully.

There might be times when you find yourself self-justifying your actions, coasting through life, wandering from your path, practicing self-deception or living in such a way that your actions don't reflect your decision to Live Deliberately. When this happens, create some kind of acronym or visual symbol to remind you to keep the 11th Commandment. You could use my S.T.A.R. acronym or create an acronym unique to your life and circumstances. Keeping the 11th Commandment adds meaning to your life by encouraging you to be honest with yourself because a life of self-deception and dishonesty will have very little real meaning.

The 2nd Key: Watch Your Thoughts - "It isn't what you have or who you are or where you are or what you are doing that makes you happy or unhappy. It is what you think about it." Dale Carnegie

The American psychologist William James believed that the greatest contribution of modern-day psychology was the idea that we can change our lives by changing our thoughts. The reason this is important is that our thoughts and beliefs determine our actions, which in turn creates our reality and experience. See Figure #2, The Mechanics of Cause & Effect. In other words, how and what you think about your life and relationship experience contributes significantly to how much meaning you will glean from that experience. "As a man thinketh in his heart, so is he." Proverbs 23:7

To illustrate how our thinking lends meaning to our experience, picture in your mind a thunderstorm soaking a farmer's drought-stricken field. The farmer sees the rain and thinks, *Ah, it's finally raining - this is good.* To the farmer, the rain means a prosperous crop. Now picture that same thunderstorm drifting a few miles away and soaking a baseball game in progress. The players see the rain and think, *Oh no, it's starting to rain – this is bad.* To the ballplayers, the rain means a cancelled game. However, the reality is that, the rain (like life itself) is neither good nor bad – the rain simply is, and the only meaning it has is the one we assign it. In the words of Shakespeare, "For there is nothing either good or bad, but thinking makes it so." Hamlet, Act 2, Scene 2

You can change the way you think by evaluating the credibility of your thoughts. One way to do this is to pause three times a day, for 90 consecutive days, and ask yourself the following question:

What thoughts have been going through my mind the past 10 minutes, and have these thoughts been distracting me from or contributing to my Flash Point Experiment?

When I practice this exercise, I am always surprised at how many of my thoughts have been negative or self-defeating. How much time I spend regretting past situations, events and relationships, worrying about future situations, events and relationships or wallowing in self-pity. In addition, I often waste time thinking about petty grievances, ridiculous scenarios or imaginary confrontations.

The 3rd Key: Practice Acorn-ness - "There can be nothing better than what you now have, and no more serious and important moment than the one you are now experiencing, because it is a real one and the only one within your power." Lev Tolstoy, *Tolstoy's Letters, Vol. 3.*

To "Practice Acorn-ness" is to live in the here and now, i.e. not regretting the past or worrying about the future. The future has yet to happen and the past no longer exists, except in your memory. Although it is natural to worry about your career, relationship and spiritual path, obsessive worry is actually a substitute for actually thinking about or dealing with what's taking place here and now. It's been said that worry is like a rocking chair - it gives you something to do but doesn't actually get you anywhere. To live in the here and now, practice Acorn-ness.

Practice Acorn-ness

Emerson once queried, "Is the acorn better than the oak tree which is its fullness and completion?" The tiny acorn already knows exactly what to do here and now in order to become a mighty oak tree in the future - absorb moisture and nutrients from the soil and send a tiny shoot to the surface. While the acorn is still a seed it doesn't worry that's it is not yet an oak tree, it focuses its energy on the essence of "acorn-ness." This allows it to progress naturally to the next stage, in this case a small sapling. Once it becomes a sapling, it doesn't regret it was once an acorn, nor does it worry that it has yet to become a tree. Instead, it focuses on the essence of "sapling-ness," and knows exactly what to do here and now - develop a solid trunk and start developing branches and leaves. This allows the sapling to progress naturally to the next stage - a beautiful oak tree. Once it becomes an oak tree, it does not regret that it is no longer a sapling, nor does it wish it was some other kind of tree, planted in some other place. Instead, it focuses on the essence of "tree-ness." It knows exactly what to do in the here and now - grow acorns, which eventually fall to the ground to repeat the growth cycle. "The past is only a memory, the future is only an expectation." British author Frank McLynn

When you live in the present and allow yourself to experience fully who or what is, or is not, in your life today, right here and right now, the future will take care of itself. Like the acorn, you will naturally progress through whatever life and relationship stages are necessary to make your life whole or complete - to become all that God knows you are capable of being. If you don't live fully present in the here and now of your existing circumstances, you will remain trapped in the Cycle of Discontent until you've accepted what or whom needs to be experienced at this stage of your life. Every time you catch yourself regretting the past or worrying about the future, "Practice Acorn-ness." In order to do this, focus on your current circumstances, career, beliefs or relationship, without wanting this experience to be any different than it actually is or desiring someone else's experience more than your own.

There are any numbers of ways you can prompt yourself to live in the here and now. For a number of years, I carried a tiny acorn in my pocket. Currently, I rely on what I refer to as Looney Tunes. You know how you frequently find some silly television jingle or popular tune continuously repeating itself in your head (those Looney Tunes). When I experience this, which for me is several times per day, I use it to remind myself to live in the present. When I hear a Looney Tune repeating itself in my head, I block out this tune by humming an uplifting hymn or stopping for a minute to say a prayer, thanking God for health and safety, and all he has done for me. In addition, I sometimes block out this these Looney Tunes by repeating a predetermined phrase, mantra or prayer to refocus my mind on the present. This phrase has changed over the years. At one time or another, I have used the following phrases:

- *The rough is only mental-* to remind myself that my thoughts determine the degree of meaning I will glean from any given experience.
- "I can do all things through Christ which strengthen me." *Philippians 4:13 –* To remind myself that God's Classroom without Walls will never provide a lesson or experience from which I have nothing to learn.
- *COME WHAT MAY -* to remind myself that I am the one who invited this life lesson, experience or solution into my life.
- "I could see peace instead of this." *(*From the book, A *Course in Miracles) -* to remind myself that I alone determine how I am going to allow myself to feel about any given circumstance, relationship or experience.
- *Show me the way -* to remind myself to stop stressing about my daily life, and shift my focus to becoming all that God knows I am capable of being.

Living in the present is critical to seeking your most essential experience, situation, or relationship because these are all states of being. You cannot *be* in the past or in the future, you can only be in your present situation. Consequently, the time spent regretting the past or worrying about the future interferes with your ability *to be* present in the moment. In the words of Christian apologist C. S. Lewis, *"*You can't go back and change the beginning, but you can start where you are and change the ending."

The 4ᵗʰ Key: Never Give Up - "Failure is the opportunity to begin again, more intelligently." Henry Ford

There are very few true dilemmas in life because a dilemma by definition is an unsolvable problem, and virtually every problem has some kind of solution (it just might not be the solution for which you were looking). Although it's true there will be many challenges on your journey through life, it is equally true there is *always* a way to get from where you are to where you need to be as long as you don't give up or quit. It's been said that Thomas Edison failed 1,000 times before he found the right filament for the light bulb he was inventing. "It is impossible to live without failing at something, unless you live so cautiously that you might as well not have lived at all." J. K. Rowling, British author

When I say, "Never Give Up," I'm not talking about staying with a toxic career, spiritual path or relationship that is leading you nowhere. This would only perpetuate The Cycle of Discontent and hinder your ability to find your most essential path. What I *am* talking about is exercising patience and not quitting. I see a distinct difference between failure and quitting. Failure is when you've tried your very best at something, but it doesn't yield the desired outcome. Quitting is the lack of will to keep trying until you succeed or fail. When you work hard at a something, but it fails, your learning is twofold; you learn what you do or what you do not want from life. In addition, if you fail to learn what works, at least you have learned what doesn't work (think of the Bill Murray character in the movie, *Groundhog Day*). However, when you quit trying before you fail or succeed, you cheat yourself out of the opportunity to learn anything. It is a key premise of Primessentialism that when you consciously strive to Advance Confidently, it is not possible to fail. Even when faced with a number of roadblocks, you will always succeed – unless you quit. I've learned that, more people quit than fail.

SUMMARY

V. EMBRACE THE EXPERIENCE: *Welcome and embrace the relationships, challenges and solutions that have come with your particular path in order to gain the insight and understanding necessary to attain a sense of meaning.*

Step 5 introduces the third component of the **Third Theme of Primessentialism**, which is to establish a sense of MEANING, by accepting, loving and embracing *all* the life lessons, relationships and experiences that come with your path. As you begin to accept your share of responsibility for everyone and everything in your life you will experience less fear, anxiety and uncertainty. You will worry less and you will begin to see how the various pieces of your life puzzle fit together. As each need is met, you will be able to see clearly, where you are and what your life is about. This clarity of meaning, coupled with a sense of purpose and direction makes your life complete, which is the **Fourth Theme of Primessentialism.** As your life becomes more balanced and complete, you experience the **Fifth Theme of Primessentialism** which is a sustainable measure of Peace & Fulfillment.

The "How" question we asked at the beginning of this chapter was, "How do I gain the insight necessary to understand why these particular lessons, ideas, circumstances and relationships that have come with my path?" The answer is simply to embrace and accept responsibility for these lessons, experiences and relationships, as well as your circumstances and station in life. The most important lesson I have learned from implementing Step 5 is that God's Classroom without Walls will continue to send the life lessons and experience I need until I've understood their significance for my life.

In addition, I've learned that, I am already where I need to be. If this were not the case, I would be someone else, experiencing something else. I have also learned that many individuals are hesitant to embrace their experience because they know in their hearts that this experience is what they really need, but they fear any change that might bring into question how they see themselves and their beliefs or challenge their lifestyle.

Now that you have been introduced to the 5-Steps, Chapter 6 will provide specific examples of how I have applied the 5-Steps to attain four of the needs most frequently expressed by our seminar participants, e.g. healthy relationships, affordable housing, meaningful work and dependable transportation.

Chapter 6

Principles to Practice

VI. Flash Point Applications

Chapters 1 through 5 introduced the Flash Point Process: 5-Steps to Peace & Fulfillment. The primary objective of Chapter 6 is to provide real-world examples of how my applying the 5-Steps has helped me to meet my own needs and solve some of the challenges and problems I have faced over the years.

"Every day is another chance to change your life." Author unknown

WHY PRACTICAL APPLICATIONS OF THE FLASH POINT PROCESS?

- Because you want to see how the Flash Point Process can help you solve your problems on a daily basis, e.g. how to attain healthy relationships, meaningful work, dependable transportation and affordable housing.

When you seek practical applications of the Flash Point Process, you're acknowledging that you're not looking for clever ideas or abstract theories, you are looking to find specific answers to the How? questions you listed at the end of the Introduction, as well as concrete solutions to your real-world problems.

MY EXPERIENCE – At the end of our seminars, we have a question and answer session during which I share my personal experience with using the Flash Point Process to meet my needs and solve my problems. I generally start this session by sharing with our seminar participants the events that led up to my Flash Point Experiment.

I often refer to this Living Skills course of instruction as a survivor's guide to purpose, direction and meaning, because, like many of my readers, I am a survivor. I have survived a dysfunctional family of origin, a bout of crippling depression, divine discontent, corporate downsizing, a divorce, a business failure, surgery, addiction issues, bankruptcy, a fractured back, four major career changes, a rare sleep disorder, broken bones, chronic nerve pain, a minor stroke, a pulmonary embolism, one tornado and a hurricane, 14 car wrecks, a heat stroke, one near-death experience and three teenage children. My point being, that my qualifications for writing this course of instruction have come from my life experience - the most brutal of all teachers.

With each life lesson, I had learned prior to, and during my Flash Point Experiment, I asked myself, *How did the lesson begin, and what steps had I taken to work through it?* I then spent the next five years thinking about all the principles I had learned from Western religion, Eastern thought, as well as a smattering of philosophy and psychology - the culmination of which became the Flash Point Process.

THE MAIN IDEAS - The purpose of this chapter is to demonstrate how the Flash Point Process can be applied to life's daily challenges, or more specifically how I applied the 5-steps to overcome some of my own challenges. In this section, you will notice that there were times when I didn't apply all 5-Steps to any given problem, and that I sometimes worked two or more steps simultaneously. I should also mention that I initially included this chapter in the book, took it out, and then put it back in. I repeated this several times before completing this book. On the one hand, I thought that real world examples of my application of the 5-Steps might possibly be insightful to my readers. On the other hand, I questioned if sharing my personal experience would be of benefit to anyone. With this in mind, I have limited this section to some of the most frequently expressed needs I have had in common with my seminar participants.

WHAT I'VE LEARNED - It would take another book to relate all that I have learned from applying the Flash Point Process to solve the problems I have encountered over the 25 years of my Flash Point Experiment. In response to those who have attended our seminars, and asked for real-life examples of how I have applied the 5-Steps to everyday challenges, I will share the following examples of how I attained:

A. Healthy Relationships

B. Meaningful Work

C. Affordable Housing

D. Dependable Transportation

A. Healthy Relationships

It's been my observation that everyone would like to have and sustain a healthy relationship. Whether these relationships be between husband and wife, parents and children, bosses and employees or neighbors with neighbors. Healthy relationships, both personal and business, are one of the cornerstones of Personal Growth because they can support and facilitate your efforts to become all you are capable of being. On the other hand, toxic relationships at best hamper that effort, and at worst, tragically derail your Flash Point Experiment.

Following my divorce, I began my dating efforts by asking God, *What's wrong with this picture?* I asked this question because I wanted to learn what had went wrong with my marriage. As anyone who has been married knows, marriage does not come with a handbook, subsequently, many first marriages fail simply due to ignorance or lack of knowledge, experience and example. When I asked this question, I realized that what I was lacking was a basic understanding of what it takes to sustain a healthy relationship, e.g. trust and intimacy, healthy boundaries, good communication skills and how to create a Mutual Support System. A Mutual Support System is one in which each party is committed to the personal growth and well-being of the other and is supportive and respectful of each other's efforts to Live Deliberately.

When petitioning God for companionship, keep in mind that what you are seeking isn't necessarily the person you are going to marry, but your next or most essential relationship for this stage of your life. For now, this could be *no* relationship, a *transitional* relationship or *the* relationship.

My first lesson from the Classroom regarding relationships began when my company hired a very attractive receptionist. I immediately sensed that there was something very special about this person. I made it a point to drop by her office every day to flirt and say hello. Since her desk was behind a tall partition, all I could see of her was from the neck up. Over the course of several weeks, I worked up the courage to ask her out for lunch. On the agreed upon day, I dropped by her office to pick her up. She smiled and greeted me when I came into her office, but when she stood up from her desk I was astonished to see that she was almost six feet tall and a very large, big-boned woman. There was no place for me to run or hide, and no way to cancel gracefully our luncheon appointment. Although I hate to admit it, I was embarrassed to be seen in public with her due to the shallowness of my personality. Consequently, I took her to an out-of-the-way restaurant, hoping that none of my friends or business associates would see us. Obviously, I had not really dropped my Checklist of Wants & Desires.

As we waited for our lunch, I decided to quit trying to be excused from this experience. I decided to embrace the woman in front of me to see what I might learn from her. Interestingly enough, it turned out that we shared a common interest in literature, art and music, and I discovered she was extremely intelligent and well-read. We formed an immediate bond of friendship and went on to enjoy a long-term relationship. In spite of my initial misgivings, this wonderful woman taught me an enormous amount about love and relationships. She provided me with the understanding and nurturing I really needed at that particular point in my life. She also scolded me (quite deservedly) for judging others by their physical appearance alone and taught me the importance of dropping my Checklist of Wants & Desires when seeking a healthy relationship.

From this experience, I learned that the relationship (or absence of one) that is most essential for me to experience, God will provide if, and when I am prepared for and receptive to that relationship and not a single day before. In other words, regardless of how impatient I might get, any effort on my part to avoid, rush or force a relationship will result in my settling for just any relationship. This always led to disillusionment or discontent.

I've also learned the importance of maintaining a high level of receptivity when it comes to personal or business relationships because of all of life's decisions, relationships tend to be most heavily influenced by our Checklist of Wants & Desires. I've learned that, I can *choose* whom I want to date, but then I have to deal with the Perils & Pitfalls of Choice. However, when I ask God to provide my next, most essential relationship, I will recognize her because our connection will be self-evident. And lastly, I've learned with certainty that there is *always* a way to find my most essential relationship if I do my part, be patient, am willing to wait, and trust God to show me the way.

B. Meaningful Work

As with most things of value, meaningful work often comes by degrees as you gain experience. What you are looking for is not so much the perfect job as you are looking for the right opportunity. This might include several less desirable jobs until you reach the point where you are qualified and ready for your most essential job or career. It could also mean you will find a project or job that is totally outside your existing career path. The amount of time it takes to bring into being your most essential career path could be a few weeks, months or several years, depending on the degree of your preparedness, the number of conduits you create, as well as the level of your receptivity. Also, keep in mind that what you are looking for is not necessarily the perfect career position, but the next work opportunity for this stage in your life.

Meaningful work is essential for Personal Growth and Physical Well-Being because it creates less stress than a meaningless work experience. In addition, it can provide financial stability, meet the physical needs of your family, as well as provide opportunities for career advancement, and introduces new skills and ideas. I have had many instances of applying the 5-Steps to finding meaningful work, and in the following pages, I will provide one example.

In 1997, I was living in San Antonio and the president of a mortgage company. I wasn't very happy with my job, so for several months, I kept asking myself why I was staying with this job. It wasn't until I got around to asking the question, *What's wrong with this picture?* that I realized I had been asking the wrong question (Step 1). What I needed to be asking was, *How can I find an opportunity that will meet my financial needs and provide a measure of fulfillment?* I tried to keep my mind open so I could see clearly what that opportunity could be, instead of thinking about what it should be (Step 2). In August of that year, I got the strangest impression from my Internal Guidance System to quit my job - strange in the sense that I didn't have another job in mind. Since I wasn't that happy with my job, I decided to heed these promptings and invited God to send me the next job, opportunity or project that was most essential for meeting the needs of my family (Step 3). I spent the next three months looking for prospects, and by the first of December I had lined up three possible new projects ("Creating the Conduits"). At this point, the impression from my Internal Guidance System to quit immediately my job became very pressing.

Unfortunately, by the end of December, all three of these new projects fell through, but the impression from my Internal Guidance System to quit my job was intensifying. I felt this so strongly that I considered quitting my job with no Plan B in place, although I realized this was not rational thinking. As I shared my predicament with my friends, they told me it would be foolish of me to quit a good paying corporate position without first having another job to replace it.

At the first of the New Year, I was going to lunch one day and felt prompted to pick up a newspaper to read. They were sold-out of my regular paper so I decided to buy a USA Today newspaper. In that particular issue was an article about a Community Builders Fellowship. This was a joint venture between Harvard University's Kennedy School of Government and the US Department of Housing & Urban Development (HUD). Interestingly enough, the instant I read this article, I recognized that this was the direction for me to pursue (Step 4). My Inner Voice clearly said, *This is next; this is it.* Although it all seemed a bit illogical at the time, I trusted God enough to submit my resignation at my job. I offered the company the option of keeping me on - not as an employee but as an independent contractor. This proved to be a win/win relationship with my former employer and simultaneously launched my career as a business consultant.

The applications for the Fellowship were due by May of 1998, with the recipients to be announced in July. Since it was only January, I still needed some kind of additional work to supplement my income from my former employer. Over the next two months, I was able to pick up two additional clients so my income never dropped below what I had been making at the mortgage company. At this point, I was more certain than ever that I was going to receive one of those Fellowships. Well, July came and went with no word from Harvard. Nonetheless, my Inner Voice continued to give me the impression that I would be awarded one of these Fellowships. By that time, my contracts with the three clients I then had were about to expire which would mean that by the end of August I would be out of work. August came and went without any word from Washington. I became very discouraged because I was struggling to embrace the possibility that I wasn't going to get a Fellowship. By late August, I was broke, emotionally and financially. Consequently, I decided to accept a job offer from a friend, but I made it clear that if by some remote possibility, I were to hear from HUD, I would be accepting that offer. I can remember being very shattered, not because I thought in any way that I deserved this Fellowship, but simply because I had felt so strongly for so long that I was going to be awarded it. This caused me to doubt my faith and question my Internal Guidance System.

When I finally quit worrying about my situation, and instead decided to embrace it (Step 5), the solution became self-evident - to call Washington in the event there had been some mistake. I called HUD and to my surprise, they said. "Where have you been; you should have responded four weeks ago, because you are supposed to be in Washington in two weeks."

This experience greatly reinforced my confidence in my Internal Guidance System and the importance of paying attention to my Inner Voice. From this experience, I learned two very important lessons. Regardless of how uncertain or illogical it might seem at first, it pays to listen to your Inner Voice, and there is *always* a way to find meaningful work. However, I extend a word of caution. The Classroom without Walls can only provide the job or career for which you are prepared and to which you are receptive. By prepared, I mean that before you find your ideal job, opportunity or career, you might need to work through several lower paying or less fulfilling jobs in order to gain the knowledge and experience necessary to land the job or find the career that is most essential for meeting your needs. By "being receptive," I mean to entertain every possible job option. When you are out of work, don't just look for a job, but also be open to looking at an opportunity or a project on which to work.

I mention project because many large corporations are no longer looking for employees because employees require the company to provide health insurance, social security benefits, stock options, retirement plans, etc. However, all corporations, as well as entrepreneurs, have projects they need to get done, and are looking for talent who will work on a contract basis. As of this writing, 20% of all Americans work on a contract basis. Many times, a project or part time job will lead to a full time job. One thing I have learned through observation and experience is that, the workplace is constantly in dire need of employees who will show up on time and have a very strong work ethic; those who do will *always* be employed.

C. Affordable Housing

I believe that everyone needs to have access to affordable housing. By affordable housing, I don't mean living in your dream house, but something that fits into your family budget at this stage of your life. The first house I owned was an old, beat up and dilapidated wood frame house on concrete blocks. I had no shame in living in such a house because, as ugly as it was, it was all that we could afford at the time. Because the house was such a wreck, we only paid $11,000 for it in 1977. We spent the next 3 years painting and repairing the house and sold it for $33,000 in 1980. I mention this because your *starter house* might be an apartment, then a mobile home and then a regular house. I've learned that, what makes a house a home is not how big it is or how expensive, but how filled it is with peace and love. There will be little peace or love is you are stressed-out about living somewhere you cannot yet afford.

In 1995, I moved from Austin to San Antonio to work on a new project. I had been living in an apartment, but since I was going to be making more money in San Antonio, I wanted to buy a house for my children. Every week I searched the classified ads to try and find a house I could afford, but with no luck. After a month of looking for a house to buy, I finally got around to asking the question, *What's wrong with this picture?* (Step1) When I did, it immediately occurred to me that I had been going in the wrong direction. Subsequently, for the next couple of weeks, I made the Commitment to See Clearly(Step 2) in order to recognize the best house for my family. I traveled all over town looking at houses to lease or lease-to-purchase. It was at that point that I that I invited God to send to me the housing that was most essential for meeting my needs. Instead of only looking for a house I could purchase, I decided to set aside my wants and desires while simultaneously trying to be receptive to any possibility (Step 3). One day, while I was searching the newspaper for a house to purchase (this was prior to Craig's List), I ran across an ad for a house that was a lease-to-purchase. As I read the ad in the paper, I felt a very strong impression that this was the house I needed for my family. In spite of this strong impression, I rejected it without looking at it. My reason for this was that the ad said it was a recently refurbished, older house. I could picture in my mind an old run down, wood frame house with window air conditioning units, so I didn't bother to go to look at it.

Oddly enough my Internal Guidance System kept giving me the distinct impression to go back and look at the lease-to-purchase house, but I decided that a clean, modern apartment would be better for my children than an old, beat-up house. That weekend I found a very clean, spacious apartment and I put money down on the first month's rent. Even after making a deposit on the apartment, I continued to feel a nagging sense that I should at least go look at that old house. I finally gave in to the promptings of my Internal Guidance System, and immediately upon driving up to that house I recognized that this was the house for my family. My Inner Voice said, *This is it; this is next* (Step 4). Instead of being an old rundown wood frame house, it was brick, freshly painted and had central air conditioning. I joyfully embraced this new reality, and when I did, it meant that I finally had a home for my family (Step 5).

Unfortunately, when I entered the house the owner was showing it to a young couple. I waited until the couple had left and told the property owner I wanted to lease his house. He apologized and said he would rather lease it to a couple than a single parent. I responded by saying, *This may seem strange, but I am certain that this is the house that is perfect for my family.* He looked at me like I was a little weird, but I told him that I was a bit of a handyman and could do any minor repairs the house might need in the coming years. He again told me he preferred to rent it to a married couple but he would sleep on it and let me know. The next morning, he called to tell me the house was mine. I later learned that this house was in a great neighborhood, close to a shopping mall and only an eleven-minute commute to my new office. God had led me to exactly where I needed to be.

A word of caution: I realize that home ownership is touted as part of the American Dream, and the money you pour into that house can be a good tax deduction. However, this is only true if it is *your* dream, and not purchased out of feeding your ego or trying fulfill the expectations of others. Home ownership does not have the allure it had 50 years ago, when the average worker stayed at their job for 30-40 years. These days, workers on average move every four years, so saddling yourself with a 30-year mortgage might not be that advantageous. From my personal experience in renting, leasing and buying houses, I've learned that there is *always* a way to find affordable housing. All you have to do is recognize it, is to pay close attention to what is going on within and around you, and trust God to guide you.

D. Dependable Transportation

By dependable transportation, I mean how you physically get from where you are to where you need to be with the appropriate vehicle to fit your budget. Over the years, I have known very intelligent, capable, well-rounded individuals whose sole mode of transportation ranged anywhere from a bicycle to city bus transportation. Although I might *want* a new car, all I really *need* is dependable and affordable transportation at this stage of my life.

Allow me to share one personal example of my applying the Flash Point Process to obtain dependable transportation. In 1994, I had been working on a project in Detroit and I was about to transfer to Austin, TX so I could be closer to my three young children who were living in Houston, TX. At the time, I was driving a car with more than 100,000 miles on it and I was going to need a more dependable car if I was going to be driving back and forth between Austin and Houston. Unfortunately, I had very little cash and I had declared bankruptcy only three years earlier so I had no idea how I was going to purchase a new car. Eventually I got around to asking God the question, *What's wrong with this picture?* (Step #1) When I did, it occurred to me that the question I needed to be asking was, *How can I acquire dependable transportation with little cash and bad credit?*

At this point, I decided to invite God to provide the means and circumstances necessary to acquire dependable transportation (Step 3). Shortly after extending this invitation, we hired an employee who was driving a new, red Pontiac Grand Prix. For some strange reason, as soon as I saw her car my Internal Guidance System gave me the impression that this was next – this was going to be the transportation I needed.

Interestingly enough, over the next few weeks my Internal Guidance System continued to give me the impression that this was the very car I needed. I shopped around used car dealerships but I could not find a used Pontiac that I could afford. Since I continued to have this nagging sense of clarity about the red car, I began to question if this was direction from my Internal Guidance System or merely my desire for that car. I decided it wouldn't cost me anything to visit a dealership and look at the new Pontiacs. When I told the salesman at the dealership that I had little cash and was fresh out of bankruptcy he said there was no way that the dealership would finance a new car for me.

About a week later the company for which I worked leased some new delivery vans and it occurred to me that maybe I could lease a car instead of buying one. I went back to the dealership and they had just acquired the very car I was looking for, and my Inner Voice said, *This is it* (Step 4). When I inquired about a lease, the salesperson told me that because of my bad credit the odds were 1,000 to one that dealer would lease me that car. I asked him to humor me and at least allow me to submit an application. This irritated him and he actually said that it would be a waste of his time because in all his years of selling cars he had never seen a lease approved with a standing bankruptcy. The next day the salesperson called me and said, "You are not going to believe this but your lease had been approved." The following day I was able to sell my old car for exactly the amount I needed to put down on the lease and drove away in my new, red Pontiac.

From this experience, I learned that God will provide the transportation we need in direct proportion to our degree of preparation and receptivity and the conduits we create. This might mean a new car, a used car, taking a bus, hitching rides with friends, riding a motorcycle or even a bicycle, depending on your needs and the degree of your receptivity. The key is to keep in mind that you will only have the transportation that meets your needs and fits your budget at this stage in your life. I realize that new car ownership is also part of the American Dream, but some individuals get so caught up in fulfilling this Dream that they sometimes over extend their budget. This happens when their purchase of a new car is heavily influenced by peer pressure and/or cultural conditioning or for the purpose of displaying their social status and feeding their ego. The point being that there is *always* a way to find dependable transportation when you pay attention to the promptings of your Internal Guidance System, listen to your Inner Voice and trust God to provide.

SUMMARY

As mentioned throughout this book, God knows "…what you stand in need of" before you ask. Consequently, the key to meeting your needs and solving your problems is to know what and how to ask. You might want a new car, home or career, but what you need is to ask for dependable transportation, affordable housing and meaningful work. You might want the perfect companion, but what is essential is the companion you need at this stage in your life.

Conclusion

I have learned that a sustainable measure of Peace & Fulfillment all boils down to whether an individual is honestly ready to ask the question, *What's wrong with this picture?* I have also learned, that this effort needs to be coupled with a sense of purpose, a commitment to see things as they really are and to seek first God's Will - COME WHAT MAY. When I exercise the courage to "Extend the Invitation," the lessons I need from the Classroom will come in direct proportion to my preparedness for, and receptivity to, that experience. As I pay conscious attention to what is going on within and around me, I will ultimately recognize the path or course of action that will provide a sense of direction. Moreover, when I exert the fearlessness necessary to embrace the ideas, relationships and events that come with this path, I will understand the significance of those experiences. This sense of meaning, coupled with a sense of purpose and direction, has made my life complete and provided me with a sustainable measure of Peace & Fulfillment.

As you apply the living skills presented in this book, your faith turns into *knowledge*, and your fear and uncertainty turn into clarity and certainty. Your need to control will be replaced with the *acceptance* that comes from trusting your Inner Voice to provide guidance and direction, confirming again and again that to do so reveals the bigger picture and the understanding necessary to complete that picture. This sense of completeness is the *confirmation* that can only come through this understanding. It's the knowledge that you are experiencing exactly what you need to end your longing and fill your void. This confirmation brings the *conviction* that the beliefs you hold are real and true, and the faith you have exercised is not blind, but is grounded in reality and Godly truths. This conviction brings the *confidence* you need to advance boldly and deliberately to the next lesson - the next crossroads in life. As you continue your efforts to Live Deliberately, in time you will ask more intently, commit more readily, invite more sincerely, pay attention more closely and embrace more freely.

The Flash Point Process is just that, a process, and it continues to evolve as I receive feedback from my readers and seminar participants. I welcome your input and comments. You can order this, and other books by Baxter Castro Coffee at www.amazon.com. If your organization would like to host a Flash Point seminar, speaking engagement or you need answers to your questions, please contact us at www.flashpointinstitute.com or write to us at: The Flash Point Institute, PO Box 690002, San Antonio, TX 78269

Appendix A
Observations on Seeing Clearly

"Knowledge lies in the investigation of things, and in seeing them as they really are. When things were thus investigated, knowledge became complete." Confucius, *The Lun Yü*

"Much is perceptible which is not perceived by us." Democritus

"What concerns me is not the way things are, but rather the way people think they are." Epictetus

"First cast out the beam out of thine own eye; and then shalt thou see clearly to cast out the mote of thy brother's eye." Jesus of Nazareth

"The great majorities of men are satisfied with appearances, as though they were realities and are often more influenced by the things that seem than by those that are." Niccolo Machiavelli, *The Prince*

"Learn how to see and remember that everything is connected to everything else." Leonardo de Vinci

"There is light enough for those who only desire to see." Blaise Pascal, Pascal's Pensées

"It is naïve to think we see things in the external world as they really are." Rene Descartes

"As a man is, so he sees." William Blake

"Imagination should be regulated by reality; instead of thinking how things may be, to see them as they are." Samuel Johnson

"The hardest thing to see is what is in front of your eyes." Johann W. Goethe

"I tried to see things as they really were, and not as I had wished them to be." Napoleon Bonaparte

"The more one looks, the more one sees" Tielhard de Chardin

"If we live truly, we shall see truly." Ralph Waldo Emerson - *Complete Essays*

"We only see what we are prepared to see." Ralph Waldo Emerson

"Many an object is not seen, though it falls within our range of vision, because it does not come within the range of our intellect, we are not looking for it. So, in the larger sense, we find only the world we are looking for." Henry Thoreau, *Walden*

"The whole secret of the study of nature lies in learning how to use one's eyes." George Sand

"The most common lie is that with which one lies to oneself. By lie I mean wishing not to see something that one does see; wishing not to see something as one sees it." Frederick Nietzsche

"I think that if we mean to do our work, the first condition is that we should not give way to fancy but look at things as they are." Lev Tolstoy

"We want to stand upon our own feet and look fair and square at the world – its good facts, its bad facts, its beauties and its ugliness; see the world as it is and be not afraid of it." Bertrand Russell

"To see clearly is poetry, prophecy and religion, all in one." John Ruskin

"We see things as we are, not as they are" Jennifer Stone

"Intelligence is the power of seeing things as they really are." George Santayana

"If we cannot see clearly, we at least want what is unclear to be in focus." Sigmund Freud

"If I could do but one thing to bless the saints it would be to give them eyes with which to see things as there are." Brigham Young

"To transform society requires the seeing of "what is,' the reality, and not what 'should be,' the illusion. I think the problem is to see clearly, then that very perception brings its own action." J. Krishnamurti

"Actualized beings have…the ability to see life clearly, to see it as it is, rather than as they wish it to be." Abraham Maslow

"I wish, above all, to make you see." Joseph Conrad

"We can only recognize what we know." E. H. Gombrich

"Seeing is a creative operation, one that demands effort." Henri Matisse

"What we see depends mainly on what we look for." John Lubbock

"The man who sees is master." Henry Ford

"We assume that to look is to see." Pablo Picasso

"We don't see things as they are we see them as we are." Anais Nin

"The simple truth of the matter is you cannot see clearly if you are controlled by preconceptions. James L. Adams

"To see in limited modes of vision is not to see at all. If you see in any given situation only what everybody else can see, you can be said to be so much a representative of your culture that you are a victim of it." S. I. Hayakawa

"We perceive, as a rule, what we expect to perceive." Peter Drucker

"Our sight really consists of a hypothesis, an interpretation of the world. We do not see the data in front of our eyes; we see an interpretation." Richard L. Gregory

"Reality for some people is broader than it is for others, because they have looked more, lived more, read more and thought more." Thomas A. Harris

"It is seeing things as they are that we can learn to change them." Tim Gallwey

"People who are suffering want to change, but they do not know how…they do not know that to bring about true healing they have to learn how to see themselves as they truly are." Mark Epstein

"The individual must be able to see reality as it truly is without biases or misconceptions." Peter Senge

"Learning only comes from seeing the world the way it really is." Chris Argyris

"Research is to see what everybody else has seen, and to think what nobody else has thought." Anon.

To see one's predicament clearly is a first step toward going beyond it." Eckhart Tolle

Acknowledgements

I am grateful for the many students and colleagues at the University of North Texas and Del Mar College who fostered in me a great love of teaching. I am also grateful for our seminar participants who provided us with the feedback and encouragement to make The Flash Point Process what it is today.

I gratefully acknowledge and express my sincere appreciation to the following individuals. Thanks to Henry Whiddon, who first encouraged me to march to the beat of my own drummer. I am also grateful to Charles Wallis for giving me the opportunity to present my first public lecture and for providing the illustrations for this book.

I would also like to thank Constance Silvestri, friend, confident and critic who helped me work through the logic and sequence of Primessentialism. I owe a very deep sense of gratitude to my children: Sarah Lynne Black, Lawrence Estlin Coffee, and Grayson Lewis Castro for their love and support, and for giving me the time and opportunity to become the kind of man they would be proud to call their father. What progress I have made in life, I owe to them. Most importantly, I express endless gratitude to my remarkable wife, Vivian, for her love, patience and editing this book.

Baxter Castro Coffee is highly sought after for his faith-based, nondenominational, Living Skills seminars. Baxter holds an MFA and is an ordained minister and motivational speaker, as well as a self-employed business consultant. He has taught seminars around the country for private and public companies, as well as faith-based organizations that serve at-risk populations.

He teaches a conceptual thinking course in Corporate America and is the author of *The Flash Point Experiment – 5 Steps to Your Most Essential Relationship,* and *The Teachings of Jesus, A Study Guide.* His critically-acclaimed, 5-Step Flash Point course has been taught through corporations, churches, drug and alcohol treatment centers, homeless shelters, and through his prison ministry. In addition, his seminars have served as part of the course curriculum for the Faith-Based Counselor Training Institute.

Baxter is a former tenured professor, and the recipient of a Community Builders Fellowship from Harvard University and HUD. He is currently the President of the Flash Point Institute.

www.ingramcontent.com/pod-product-compliance
Lightning Source LLC
Chambersburg PA
CBHW060253100426
42742CB00011B/1736